The

Baby Signing Bible

ADELANTE

AVERY   a member of Penguin Group (USA) Inc.   New York

The
Baby
Signing
Bible

Baby Sign Language Made Easy

Laura Berg

founder and president of My Smart Hands®

Published by the Penguin Group
Penguin Group (USA) Inc., 375 Hudson Street, New York, New York 10014, USA • Penguin Group
(Canada), 90 Eglinton Avenue East, Suite 700, Toronto, Ontario M4P 2Y3, Canada (a division of Pearson
Penguin Canada Inc.) • Penguin Books Ltd, 80 Strand, London WC2R 0RL, England • Penguin Ireland,
25 St Stephen's Green, Dublin 2, Ireland (a division of Penguin Books Ltd) • Penguin Group (Australia),
250 Camberwell Road, Camberwell, Victoria 3124, Australia (a division of Pearson Australia Group Pty
Ltd) • Penguin Books India Pvt Ltd, 11 Community Centre, Panchsheel Park, New Delhi–110 017,
India • Penguin Group (NZ), 67 Apollo Drive, Rosedale, North Shore 0632, New Zealand (a division of
Pearson New Zealand Ltd) • Penguin Books (South Africa) (Pty) Ltd, 24 Sturdee Avenue, Rosebank,
Johannesburg 2196, South Africa

Penguin Books Ltd, Registered Offices: 80 Strand, London WC2R 0RL, England

Most Avery books are available at special quantity discounts for bulk purchase for sales promotions,
premiums, fund-raising, and educational needs. Special books or book excerpts also can be created to fit
specific needs. For details, write Penguin Group (USA) Inc. Special Markets, 375 Hudson Street, New York,
NY 10014.

Library of Congress Cataloging-in-Publication Data

Berg, Laura.
The baby signing bible : baby sign language made easy / Laura Berg.
p.   cm.
ISBN 978-1-58333-471-3
1. Nonverbal communication in infants.   2. Interpersonal communication in infants.   3. Infants—
Language.   4. Sign language.   I. Title.
BF720.C65B47   2012   2012013681
419'.1—dc23

Printed in the United States of America
10   9   8   7   6   5

BOOK DESIGN BY NICOLE LAROCHE

While the author has made every effort to provide accurate telephone numbers, Internet addresses, and
other contact information at the time of publication, neither the publisher nor the author assumes any
responsibility for errors, or for changes that occur after publication. Further, the publisher does not have
any control over and does not assume any responsibility for author or third-party websites or their content.

This book is dedicated to my mom. She was an amazing role model who always believed in me. I only wish to be as good a mom to my children as she was to me. I also want to dedicate this book to my children, who were my inspiration to begin my signing journey. And finally, to my husband, the most amazing man in the world.

Contents

· ·

Introduction

· ·

My passion for baby sign language stems from both a personal and an educational place. I was a schoolteacher before starting My Smart Hands, a company that teaches parents how to communicate with their preverbal babies using American Sign Language. While in teachers' college, I happened to take an American Sign Language (ASL) course as my second-language credit. I fell in love. I loved being able to communicate in a nonverbal way. It was refreshing going to classes and spending three hours not speaking or vocalizing in any way. I loved how physically expressive you had to be, using your whole body and face to communicate. ASL took me out of my comfort zone, challenged me, and ultimately intrigued me so much that I continued to take ASL courses as the years went on. Eventually I ended up with a certificate in ASL and Deaf Studies.

When I became a teacher, I was asked to run the literacy program at our school. We had a group of students who were really struggling with spelling and reading comprehension. The traditional curriculum wasn't working, and I felt we needed a fresh approach. I did an enormous amount of research on literacy and came upon a study that used the ASL alphabet to help students learn their spelling words. I was fascinated. This mode of instruction made so much sense to me, and I wanted it to make sense to my students.

As teachers we are encouraged to use the VAK (Visual, Auditory, and Kinesthetic) method of teaching. Each class always has a broad range of learners, and by using these three modes of instruction, the theory goes, a teacher can cover all learning styles. If a child tends toward a kinesthetic (physical or tactile) style of learning, for example, it might be difficult for him to learn his spelling words. He needs to experience his learning in a physical way. If he was trying to learn his words by sight or by hearing alone, his efforts wouldn't register in the area of his brain where his learning strength lies. Using ASL letters to teach spelling, however, allows that child to feel or experience the letters in a different way, which in turn opens up a different mode of learning. Using ASL in a classroom is visual (the child can see the sign or letter), auditory (we always combine voice with the sign), and kinesthetic (the child can experience the sign through the body). The ASL for literacy program was hugely successful. At the outset, I had students who were regularly getting eight or nine right out of twenty on their spelling tests. After learning their spelling words using the ASL alphabet, their test scores improved to eighteen or nineteen out of twenty.

Two years later, I began guest lecturing at a number of universities across Canada—speaking to teacher education programs on the benefits of using sign language to promote literacy. During my research for these lectures, I came across numerous articles and studies on baby sign language. I learned that sign language offers babies a way to communicate with those around them. And it makes sense—they are constantly gesturing and they learn to wave bye-bye and blow kisses at a very early age. Signing builds on these natural developments and gives babies the tools they need to communicate.

I knew I would teach my own baby sign language when the time came. In 2005, my husband and I welcomed a beautiful baby girl into the world. I began signing with her when she was four months old. Fireese was nine and a half months old when she finally signed "milk," and I was beyond excited. At eleven months, her signing exploded, and by twelve months she was using more than thirty signs on a regular basis. It was so wonderful to have her communicate her needs to me so easily and without frustration.

My personal signing "aha" moment came when Fireese was ten months old. She was sitting in her high chair, snacking on Cheerios. She kept signing "more" but was then throwing her Cheerios on the floor. Frustrated by the mixed message and the mess, I said, "If you don't want more Cheerios, what do you want?" She signed "more" and "cheese." I was amazed for two reasons. First, my ten-month-old baby had put two words together. That clearly showed me that she had a greater word comprehension and more complex thought process than I had realized. Second, she had made her wishes perfectly clear. I would never have known what she wanted if she hadn't signed to tell me. I hadn't offered her cheese during that snack, nor was there any cheese in sight. I would have assumed that she was finished eating and put her down. At that point she likely would have thrown a temper tantrum because she wasn't done; she simply wanted something salty versus something sweet. That was my big moment—one I could use to prove to other parents that signing works, and can work incredibly well.

I have had some older generations of parents tell me that they always knew what their babies wanted. My response is always,

"No, you knew what your child didn't want." There's a big difference between knowing what a child doesn't want and knowing what he does want. I knew my daughter didn't want Cheerios, but if she hadn't been able to sign, I wouldn't have known she *wanted* cheese. Instead she was able to easily and confidently tell me what she wanted.

It was my passion for baby signing that led me to create My Smart Hands. I wanted to share this great form of communication with other parents. Because of my background as a curriculum specialist, it was very easy for me to create an engaging program for parents to follow. I made sure that our classes were full of music, stories, and games. Over the years, I've posted more than three hundred signing videos on YouTube. I receive e-mails every day from parents all over the world asking for advice on how to sign with their baby. Many of these parents can't access My Smart Hands classes in their location. I've been asked thousands of times if I have a book that parents can learn from at home. *The Baby Signing Bible* is that book.

After years of developing the My Smart Hands signing program and teaching thousands of families how to sign with their babies, I can now share my expertise with new parents everywhere. I know that signing with your child will make your life and your baby's life much easier, and the feeling of witnessing your baby's first "sign" is beyond magical. Your little one will have the tools she needs to tell you what she wants. You'll find this book to be an easy-to-follow, step-by-step guide to successfully signing with your child. I've included interesting stories from signing parents, as well as fun tips, to help you incorporate signing into your daily routines. You'll gain the ability to teach your child to let you know what he *does* want. Both of you will be much happier as a result.

Part I

The
Basics

An Introduction to Baby Sign Language

B efore you learn how to sign with your baby, you may want to learn a bit about American Sign Language (ASL) itself. ASL has a fascinating history and development as a language. One point that people always find interesting about American Sign Language is that it is unique to North America. All countries, even English-speaking ones, have their own sign language. If you know ASL, you won't be able to communicate with people from Britain because they use British Sign Language (BSL). Even deaf people who travel abroad won't necessarily be able to communicate with other deaf people unless they know the other sign language. So ASL is more unique to America than even English. Another interesting point is that ASL is a language unto itself. Some people think it is a direct translation of English, but it is actually very different. The sentence structure, grammar use, and syntax are not like the English language. I hope you find this brief history of ASL interesting.

The History of ASL

ASL began as the result of Thomas Hopkins Gallaudet's interest in teaching his neighbor's deaf daughter. He had discovered that she was a smart little girl despite the fact that she couldn't speak or hear. He became interested in learning how to go about formally teaching this little girl and other deaf children. In 1814 he raised enough money to go to Europe, where there was a history of deaf education. He wanted to see if there were standard teaching methods for those who were deaf. There he met a Frenchman named Laurent Clerc, a teacher at the National Institute for Deaf-Mutes. Gallaudet asked Clerc to come back to America with him to help him develop a school for the deaf. In 1817 they founded the American School of the Deaf in West Hartford, Connecticut, which at that time was known as the Connecticut Asylum for the Education and Instruction of Deaf and Dumb Persons.

Before ASL was developed, deaf people had used home signs. Home sign language was a simple set of hand gestures that allowed basic communication between the members of a family. Think of it like charades. Family members would act out an idea that they were trying to get across. Eventually, they would develop common gestures or signs that they could use on a regular basis.

The exception to this was Martha's Vineyard, a small island in Massachusetts, where an unusual number of people were born deaf. Consequently, a local sign language started to develop there, which later became known as Martha's Vineyard Sign Language (MVSL). Interestingly, it was used by both deaf and hearing people. Because Martha's Vineyard was a small, tight-knit community, even hearing people found it useful to learn sign language. No one knows for sure why there was such a high rate of deafness in Martha's Vineyard. Historians speculate that it was due to its isolation from mainland America. There would have been a couple of people who had the deaf gene, and over the years that gene would have been passed down from generation to generation. It is a small island, so people may have married others who shared the same ancestor several generations back. Because of that, they would both have the recessive deaf gene, therefore passing it on to their children.

Many children from Martha's Vineyard attended the American School of the Deaf when it opened, only to find that a good number of the teachers were more fluent in French Sign Language (FSL) than in home signs or MVSL. This school was one of the first opportunities for deaf people to come together to be educated. The bringing together of different sign languages allowed for teachers and pupils to combine the best and most logical of all the gestures they had been using. The consistency of being together and the formality of education allowed common signs to develop. Deaf students would then bring these signs home and use them with their friends and family members all over the United States. The combination of the formal education and merging of several sign languages eventually led to the development of ASL.

Even though ASL was commonly used as a language in its own right—with its own grammar and syntax, as well as its own idioms and culture—it wasn't always acknowledged as a formal language until the early 1960s. In the mid-1950s, William Stokoe, an English professor who worked at Gallaudet University, began his extensive research on ASL and managed to convince critics and experts alike that American Sign Language was a natural language on the same level as any other language. In 1960 Stokoe published a monograph titled "Sign Language Structure," a paper published at the University of Buffalo that analyzed the language of ASL. It's a language that uses a combination of hand shapes, facial expressions, and body movements rather than a combination of sounds. As such, sign language is also referred to as "manual" language. Thanks to Stokoe, many universities now offer ASL as a foreign language credit.

Signing with Babies

Baby sign language has been around for as long as deaf people have been having children. Baby signing initially developed as a way to help hearing babies communicate with deaf parents and siblings. Dr. Joseph Garcia was the first man to observe and research baby sign language, which he began studying in 1975. While attending the University of Alaska, he developed a passion for how communication could exist between people with hearing difficulties as opposed to those who did not have a hearing difficulty. Dr. Garcia's passion for baby sign language was mainly triggered when he noticed that the babies of his friends, who were deaf, could still communicate with their parents.

Through further research, Dr. Garcia noted that while babies with hearing parents cannot communicate much by the ninth month, babies with deaf parents could express their needs through the use of sign language. He found that it was much easier for babies to make gestures with their hands than it was to form words with their tongues. The muscles needed to produce a sign with their hands developed much sooner than the small muscles of the tongue required to form words and was therefore a much easier way for a baby to communicate. Dr. Garcia finalized his thesis on sign language interaction in 1986. Based on his research, Dr. Garcia held that teaching babies how to sign from around six to seven months of age improves the linguistic ability of hearing babies, jump-starting development.

Experts are now discovering that babies who sign at an earlier age (newborn and onward) may be able to begin signing back to you at the six-month mark. It is never too early or too late to start signing with your little one. Even once your baby begins to speak words, she may not say all words clearly. Signing, even with a child who has started talking, will still be useful to help avoid the frustration of you not understanding what your child is saying. If a word is unclear, you can ask for the sign and then you'll easily be able to understand what your child is saying.

I started signing with both of my children when they were around four months old. I felt that at this time they were able to focus on me and I could hold their attention for a few seconds. My daughter started signing back to me when she was nine and a half months old; my son, Hartford, when he was six months old. If I had waited to start signing with my son until he was six months, then I would have possibly missed out on weeks or months of him being able to communicate to me through signs.

Choosing ASL vs. Making Up Your Own Signs

When choosing to sign with your baby, there are many reasons to use ASL rather than making your own signs. The first reason is its availability. Believe it or not, many people today know at least a little sign language. You probably know at least a few words yourself. Dr. Marilyn Daniels, author of *Dancing with Words: Signing for Hearing Children's Literacy,* states: "There are nearly 15 million people in North America able to communicate to some degree in sign language, making it the third most commonly used language in the country." ASL is mostly used in the United States and English-speaking parts of Canada but also in some areas of Mexico.

Why make up your own signs that you'll have to remember and will not find use for in the future when there is already a full language of signs available? If you start to teach your child a sign and then you forget that sign, you can easily find that sign online or in a book. If you've made up the sign, then there is no way to look it up. This helps with being consistent when teaching signs to your little one. ASL is a full and beautiful language that is used by millions of people across North America.

Some researchers are in favor of making up your own signs, arguing that many ASL signs are too difficult for babies. I have not found this to be the case, and neither have millions of other parents. American Sign Language is an extension of the gestures that babies do naturally. For example, the sign for dog is patting your leg like you are calling the dog to you. This is an easy and natural sign for a child to make. Never underestimate your little one's abilities. He may not make the signs perfectly at first, but he will certainly try. It's just like when babies start talking, they may not say the words perfectly but they eventually get there.

As your baby grows older your child will probably see ASL being used on *Sesame Street* or other children's programs or in the community where you live. It's exciting for toddlers to see signing being done in the world around them. And with more and more deaf children being mainstreamed into regular classrooms, many hearing children will have the opportunity to meet and become friends with deaf peers.

You may also find that your child's babysitter, day care worker, or teacher knows many basic signs and can therefore communicate with your toddler as well as you can. This is even more exciting for your little one to realize that not only do his mom and dad understand him, but other people do too.

What About Signs That Have No Exact Translation?

Since ASL is a language in and of itself and not an extension of the English language, there is often not an exact sign for an English word. In ASL, just a few signs can convey a full English sentence. This is because of the body movement and facial expressions that also make up part of ASL. By the same token, a single English word may have no exact translation, and in this case the word is often spelled out with your hands using the ASL alphabet; this is referred to as "finger spelling."

I remember when my daughter first started eating, one of her favorite foods was yogurt. At the time, I asked my ASL teacher what the sign for yogurt was, and he told me it was finger spelled. Once I had my son, I was looking up a sign online and came across a great dictionary in which I found the sign for yogurt. I then asked the same ASL teacher who I had since become friends with about the sign "yogurt" and he told me that there is now a consensus of the use of this new sign in the deaf community. He has found that since the availability of online resources and communication tools such as YouTube, the ASL language is adding new words at a faster pace than previously. Of course it's not recommended that hearing people make up signs in ASL. It's when large groups in the deaf community have come to agree upon the use of the new sign that it becomes accepted. There is no formal acceptance process when new signs are created; there is no deaf group that gets together and comes up with new signs. Rather, it happens organically when people in a community see the need to create a new sign for a word that is used frequently.

Whenever I came across a word that was finger spelled—for example, broccoli—I would always say to my daughter, "Broccoli starts with the letter *b*, *b* is for broccoli." This way I wasn't making up signs, and I could always remember what I used for that sign.

If you choose to use proper American Sign Language when learning to sign with your baby, you will quickly build up a vocabulary that grows with practice. Basic communication with a deaf individual definitely becomes possible through the use of your elementary signing vocabulary, similar to how travelers communicate with the locals in foreign-speaking countries. With time, when you learn the language, you'll be able to communicate with the deaf or hard of hearing through a mutual language you both understand.

Parents who take My Smart Hands classes often ask if they will be able to communicate with deaf people. I always point out that when learning any language, you start with a very basic vocabulary, but you can still communicate on an elementary level. One day, when I first started learning ASL, I ran into a deaf person in the mall food court. I saw that she was having trouble communicating to the food vendor what she wanted on her sandwich. I went up and asked her what was wrong and if I could help by using the basic signs "wrong" and "help." I had yet to learn how to form full sentences in ASL, but I knew my basic vocabulary could potentially help.

The woman told me she wanted more sauce; I understood the word "more" but not the word "sauce." I asked her to finger spell "sauce" using the alphabet signs, which she did. I was then able to tell the food vendor that the woman wanted more sauce on her sandwich. She thanked me for my help. I felt good that I was able to assist the hearing food vendor who was unable to understand the deaf person—and at the same time I learned a new sign— "sauce." Even with my limited repertoire of signs, I was able to communicate on a basic level with a deaf person.

Learning baby sign language is a great foundation for learning full ASL as a second language. I think that, as with any language, if you try to speak to a person in their native tongue, they appreciate your efforts to communicate with them so personally. You can definitely consider this a great starting point to a lifetime of learning this wonderful, growing language. The beauty of signing with your baby is that you don't need to be fluent, or even know any signs at all, to be able to do it successfully. You can easily learn one word at a time, at the same pace as your baby. Before you know it, you will have a nice repertoire of signs.

Is Sign Language Universal?

People often assume that sign language is the same all around the world. This is not true. Just like spoken languages, sign language is different from country to country. Even more interesting is that in other English-speaking countries sign language is different. For example, British Sign Language (BSL) is very different from ASL. Not only does sign language vary from country to country, but it can even vary from region to region. This is known as a sign dialect. I know at least five different ways to sign "happy birthday" depending on where you live. Many new learners of ASL get confused by the fact that there are different signs for the same word. I point out to them that this is the same in the English language. Sometimes it depends on what region you're in, or what words you use for certain things. For example, some people may order a soda, or pop, or a Coke; all of those words basically mean the same thing, it just depends on which area of the country you've grown up in.

As you're learning ASL and you come across different ways to sign the same word, it doesn't mean that one is wrong; it just means that the author or illustrator may be in a different region from the one in which you've learned. Just pick which sign feels right for you and use that one.

The Benefits of Teaching Children Sign Language

Now that you know a little about the history of ASL and signing with babies, let's take a closer look at the benefits of teaching your child this amazing language. There are many more than you may realize, including early communication; less frustration; mutual happiness and a strong bond; higher IQ; brain development and advanced language skills; high self-esteem and confidence; and, most important, fun.

Communication

How many times have you wished you could gather one tangible want or need from your baby's cries? Your inability to understand your child and his attempts to express himself are frustrating for both of you. Communication begins as soon as a baby is born, and it is critical for building a connection between parent and child. But a baby has various natural limitations when it comes to communicating. Of course, you can't expect your baby to say, "Mommy, I am thirsty." He expresses his desires through body language, facial expressions, and verbal sounds. It takes time for these movements and expressions to evolve into a language you can understand. And until that happens, you need to try your best to understand what your infant is telling you.

Babies are able to make gestures and movements with their hands long before their mouths are able to form words. The gross motor skills (large muscles) involved in making a sign are much easier for a baby than the fine motor skills (small muscles) needed for the mouth and tongue to form words. This makes it easier for a baby to begin to communicate with sign language than with spoken language.

Babies *want* to communicate with you. They try to mimic the sounds you make. They wave their hands to try to attract your attention. They point at things when they want something. Have you ever seen a baby who is simply ecstatic about clapping his hands? He's excited because his actions—the clapping—have gotten a positive response from you. Have you ever seen a child proud of himself for waving bye-bye? The pride comes from his ability to participate in the social interaction that is happening at that time.

This is why signing is so beneficial. Babies have so much more to say to us than words will allow. These little people are amazingly smart, and teaching them to sign allows them to express their intelligence in unexpected ways.

When you teach your child signs, it helps to bridge the communication gap that exists before words come into play. Signing allows your baby to use his brain and communicate his thoughts to you before he can talk. And because your child is now able to communicate, you as the parent tend to give him more language to use. It's a beautiful circle: the more he shows he knows, the more words you give him, and the more words he learns, the more he can communicate.

Less Frustration

Giving your baby the tools to communicate through the use of signs can help bridge the frustrating language stage between the ages of four months and two and a half years, a period when your baby wants to communicate but his ability to speak is non-existent or limited. What if you were feeding your baby peas when he really wanted a banana, and he was unable to tell you? He would become incredibly frustrated with you and possibly with the situation. Telling you that he doesn't want peas is easy: he can spit them out or refuse the spoon. But how can he tell you what it is that he *does* want? If your child has the use of signs, he could easily sign "banana," alleviating all the guesswork and frustration. Adding signs to a baby's language bank not only leads to more effective communication, but it also offers a bridge of words for babies when learning to talk, thereby reducing frustration. I will discuss more thoroughly in chapter 6 how signing can help a child when learning to talk.

Hurt Foot
· ·

When my daughter was around ten months old, I decided to teach her the sign for hurt. I almost didn't teach her the sign because I figured that she could easily point to whatever was hurting when I asked her to. But she was teething really badly at this time, and so it was a way for me to sympathize with the pain that she was experiencing by making the sign "hurt" in front of my mouth. I was glad that I taught her this sign when one day we were going outside for a walk and it was so cold out, I wanted to put socks and running shoes on her. She hated wearing socks and running shoes, and we were just coming off the summer when she had been able to wear sandals or go barefoot. During this transition time she would always fight me when I tried to put her socks or her shoes on. This one day she seemed especially angry with me, and she was fighting me and crying and pulling at her sock. We were running late and I was getting frustrated with her; all I wanted her to do was put her shoes on. Once I finally won and got her shoes on, she looked at me with the saddest expression on her face and quietly signed "hurt" over her toe. I took off her shoe and her sock only to find out a tiny little piece of cat litter was stuck in between her toes and was clearly hurting her foot. I felt terrible that I was forcing the little munchkin to put her shoes on when all she was doing was trying to tell me that her foot hurt. I was glad that she was able to tell me that she was hurting, since I was just assuming that she was being difficult.

—LAURA BERG

. . . .

Mutual Happiness and Strong Bond

A baby who can easily communicate his needs to you will, in general, be much happier because he can make himself understood. And when babies are happier, parents are happier too. As a parent, there is nothing more upsetting than to have your child look at you with sadness because you don't understand what he wants. Take my earlier example about the baby who is frustrated because his mom doesn't understand that he wants a banana and not peas. Imagine that baby easily being able to ask for the banana and you not having to go through the guessing game of trying to figure out what he wants. Would you be much happier enjoying a peaceful mealtime as opposed to dealing with a crying baby?

A happy and contented baby creates a strong bond with his parents. When my daughter was born, she was the happiest and most good-natured baby. We bonded easily, as she was always smiling and cooing at me; it was lovely. When I had my son, however, he had the worst case of colic I'd ever seen. My husband and I said that he had two states of being: asleep and miserable. It was a brutal stretch of time, and I found that bonding with him was more difficult. I felt like I couldn't do anything right for this poor little kid. Then one day, almost overnight, the colic went away and the happy baby arrived. It felt like a miracle. After that it was so much easier to bond with him, as most of our anxiety was gone. The same applies to children who become frustrated and even throw temper tantrums because they can't be understood. If you take those tense times out of the equation, then you are able to develop a strong bond with each other.

Higher IQ, Brain Development, and Language Skills

Research studies have shown that using sign language can boost a child's IQ. This is because of the early brain work that babies do when they are exposed to sign language. When you teach a young child sign language, you are exercising a different portion of his brain than you do when you simply give him a spoken language. The baby takes signs in as an image on the visual side of his brain, whereas when you speak to him, he takes those words in on the auditory portion of his brain. Similar to when you read aloud together with a child, you are giving the child both visual and verbal cues. When you use words and signs together, you are exercising a larger portion of the brain. When I first began researching sign language use for hearing children, I was amazed to learn this. We, as humans, use such a small portion of our brain in our everyday lives. There is definitely room for more "brainpower" usage.

When babies are able to communicate through the use of sign language, they are able to use a broader vocabulary than babies who are still not able to use words. If your child has a number of signs to draw from, you can ask a question like "What would you like to eat?" as opposed to the more limiting "Would you like Cheerios?" This gives the child the ability to think about what he wants, think about his choices, and then answer you through a sign. You are allowing your child to have a more elaborate thought process. If your child does not have the ability to tell you specific things, then you may ask your child if he wants A or B, giving him a choice between two things versus asking him what he wants. This does not allow for the same thought process as the first option. And because he is able to communicate more complicated thoughts to you, you end up giving him more language to use. When he does start to speak, he will do so with a larger vocabulary. After all, he's been using language for a longer time than a child who has not been using sign language.

Our daughter, Fireese, is now in the first grade and reads at a grade-three level. She is very proud of the fact that she is already learning complex math skills such as her times tables. She is also teaching herself to play the guitar. I really think that teaching her sign language helped her brain development at an early age. There was an interesting study done by the University of Oregon led by Aaron J. Newman, who looked at sign language and the brain. Normally people learn language using the left side of their brain. But the study found that when a person learns sign language as a baby, they use a portion of their right brain called the right angular gyrus, which is often associated with creativity. The researchers tested twenty-seven people, eleven of whom had learned sign language as a baby. During the ASL portion of the test, the volunteers who had learned the language as babies had their right angular gyrus light up versus the people who had not. Perhaps the early exposure to sign language helped my daughter with her early creativity, as the right side of her brain was exercised through the use of ASL.

Higher Self-Esteem and Confidence

As I mentioned earlier, sign language provides your child with tools to express himself before he can speak. What better way to help build self-esteem than by being able to comprehend and engage in what your little one is saying to you or asking you for. The child who is able to communicate with others feels relaxed and secure because he can make himself understood.

Dr. Garcia once told me a great story that stuck with me as a teacher and parent:

There was once a little boy in a day care who knew how to sign. One day while the teachers were getting the milk and cookies ready for snack time, the children were getting fussy and whining for their cookies. One little boy who could sign walked up to the teacher and looked her square in the eye and confidently signed "cookie." The teacher looked at this little boy and smiled and gave him his cookie. The reason this little boy was given his cookie was because he was asking in a polite manner. He wasn't crying or screaming for his snack. All of the little kids around him were amazed that this little boy was able to get his cookie so easily. For the rest of the day the teachers watched the interaction of the other kids with this little boy. All of the other children seemed to look up to this little boy and were following him around, going from station to station. Wherever this little boy would go, they would follow.

All the children looked up to the little boy because he easily got a cookie from his day care teacher. He was able to get the cookie because he clearly and calmly communicated what he wanted and therefore he was seen as somebody to look up to by his peers. This gave him great confidence in the classroom, which in turn led to high self-esteem.

The first time I heard this story I was amazed. Then I realized that it made complete sense. I saw this with my daughter when I began signing with her. Before she picked up the signs, I could see her getting very frustrated trying to communicate with me. After she learned a few signs to use, I noticed that she was a lot more confident in her environment. She could easily tell me what she wanted, and I would respond to her. This eliminated a lot of the guesswork I had to do and made her a confident little baby because she was able to clearly communicate with me and with those around her.

Supporting Independence

When my daughter was younger and I would take her to a play place, I felt like I had to walk a fine balance between letting her explore her environment and making sure that she was okay and didn't need help. I wanted to help her develop her confidence as well as her socializing skills. I remember one time when we were at a play center and she was playing with this one toy when another little girl came up to her and took the toy away. My mommy gut reaction was to immediately go over there and get the toy back for my daughter. But instead I waited to see my daughter's reaction, to see if she needed any help. I looked at her and signed "help," and she shook her little head "no." Then she reached over and took the toy back from the little girl. I thought this was great—she was able to deal with the situation with another little child—when all of a sudden this little girl again took the toy away from my daughter. Then my daughter turned and took the toy back. Then this little girl turned and hit my daughter in the head. Of course, at this point I got up and went to mediate the situation, but as I was walking over to my daughter, she started making the sign "help." I thought this was very cool to see that I initially offered her help and she said no, and

then when she genuinely did want my help, she was able to eas-
ily look at me and request it. Signing was great in this case be-
cause it allowed me to allow my daughter to experience the world
around her while having the security of easily being able to ask
me for help when she needed it.

—TARA M.

. . . .

Signing Is Fun!

Aside from all the other wonderful benefits of signing, it's fun. Signing adds an element to your life that's not only a great educational
tool but is also really enjoyable. When you read a story with your
child, you may ask him to point to a picture to engage him. When
you read and sign to your little one, he becomes much more involved in the experience, making it more fun. You may ask him to
point to a picture and then ask him to show you the sign for the
picture. You can show him the sign and ask him to copy you or
you can help him make it. This is a fun process for children because
the learning becomes more active (showing signs) versus passive
(simply listening).

You can also play fun signing games with your child (see games
section in chapter 8). My daughter's favorite game was "guess the
letter." I would hold up my hand and show her a letter and she
would have to guess what it was. Once she got it, then it was her
turn to hold up a letter and my turn to guess. When she grew older,
we would put the sounds to the letters. She'd have to make the

sound instead of saying what the letter was. When she became even older we would string the letters together to form words. This was one way she learned how to read. She wasn't interested in looking at written letters on a page, but making the letters with her hands fascinated her.

The best thing about signing is that it's always with you. You don't need to bring anything along to use it. If you're at a restaurant and you're waiting for your food, you can play a game of "guess what I am signing." It's easy and entertaining. You'll definitely enjoy using signing for more than a simple communication tool.

Sign Language and Speech Development

"Will sign language hinder my child's speech development?" This is the number one burning question when it comes to teaching your baby how to sign. It's natural to have such a concern, but there is no need to worry.

Research has shown that signing does not interfere with speech development; in fact, the opposite holds true. Using sign language can actually help facilitate children's language development. People confuse speech and language. A child can have and use meaningful language without speech.

I always give parents this example: Take two children who are both late talkers; you've signed with one but not the other. The child who you've signed with will have a larger vocabulary when he starts to speak, because he's been using complex language through the use of signs. The child you didn't sign with will have a more limited vocabulary. If a parent doesn't know how much their child truly comprehends, they may keep their spoken language overly simple. This child will have much further to go to catch up to his peers when his speech develops. Children aren't lazy; they want to talk. When they develop the ability to talk, they will do so nonstop. Additionally, one thing does not cause the other. Signing with your child does not cause him to be a late talker. He would have been a late talker regardless, and you are helping him by giving him more complex language to use even before he begins to speak. Sign language provides children with an earlier access to language, thus establishing a foundation for more vocabulary-building experiences.

There are different studies to support the fact that kids exposed to several languages, including sign language, achieve a higher language competency at an early age.

A section of the National Institutes of Health, the Eunice Kennedy Shriver National Institute for Child Health and Human Development, studied 140 families with eleven-month-old babies. They compared babies of families that used signs with those that did not. In all the tests, the children in the families that used signs performed better than the children whose families did not use signs. They scored higher in intelligence tests, understood more words, had larger vocabularies, and engaged in more sophisticated play.

Speech vs. Language

Speech is the sound we use to produce words. It is the mechanics—how your lip and tongue muscles move to form words and how air flows through your larynx to create sound.

Language is a system for communicating. It could be voice sounds (speech), gestures (signs), or written symbols.

You can use and understand language without speech.

How to Deal with Skeptics

Whenever I teach parents how to sign with their babies, I always address the myth that signing can delay speech. I say this not for the sake of the class participants (they are obviously there because they're excited to sign with their babies), but rather for the naysayers they may encounter. I like to give parents the ammunition they need to be able to quash these types. Additionally, I have some parents ask me how to convince day care workers, grandparents, babysitters, or other caregivers to sign with their baby.

There are some people who may be skeptical about teaching a baby how to sign. They believe that teaching infants sign language will cause them to be lazy when it comes to talking. This is not true (as discussed above), but you may find yourself having to explain this from time to time. I always think it's funny when people tell me that their neighbor's granddaughter's best friend's cousin signed with her daughter and she was a late talker. Whenever I've actually run into someone whose child was a late talker and had been exposed to sign language, they've always acknowledged the fact that they were very happy that they used sign language or otherwise their child would have had no form of communication. These people realize that using sign language did not cause the speech delay, but rather gave the child a meaningful language to use until her speech developed.

It's also important for you to feel confident in telling caregivers about the signs your baby knows and uses. If your little one tries signing to a babysitter and she doesn't understand her, it will cause her undue frustration. Remember, this is your child and the caregiver should respect your child-rearing wishes. You have the right as the parent to ask the caregiver to use a communication tool that your child uses. This will make the caregiver's life easier as well as your child's.

What you may want to tell the people in your signing baby's life:

1. Signing babies can develop language skills earlier than babies who never learn to sign. This makes earlier communication much clearer and easier.

2. Signing greatly reduces temper tantrums because the infant can communicate a need or want before he can talk. Signing removes much of the guesswork from figuring out what your baby wants.

3. Babies who sign tend to be less frustrated and happier, making for happier parents. This helps a strong bond form between baby and parent.

4. Babies who learn sign language develop recall skills that make them better performers at school later on. Because of

the early exposure to language, signing babies are able to use a larger portion of their brain.

5. Signing enables a child to share his thoughts and interests before he can talk. This creates a confident child with higher self-esteem. He's not worried about being misunderstood.

6. The most important reason to sign with your baby is that it's so much fun. Children just love using sign language and are excited to be able to communicate. Signing games add another rich element to family life. You'll quickly see how children enjoy signing.

Baby Signing in Bilingual Households

People often ask me if using two spoken languages and adding signs to the mix will confuse the baby.

When a baby first starts learning about language, she makes a one-to-one correlation between a word and the object/action that it stands for. For instance, a baby in an English-only environment will make the following correlation—the white stuff in my bottle is milk. However, the scenario is different when a baby is in a bilingual environment, as she will have two labels to choose from. For instance, a baby from a Spanish/English environment will recognize both milk and *leche*. But because she will make a one-to-one correlation, she will most likely use one word rather than both. For her, the white stuff in her bottle is either milk or *leche*.

This is where signing comes in handy. By providing your baby with one visual sign for *leche* and milk, you are linking the object with both these words. This makes it easier for the baby to understand. For instance, if your baby hears the word "*leche*" when this is paired with the sign used for the word "milk," the result is, "Wow, they mean the same thing!" The bottom line: sign language speeds up the process of recognizing different words with the same meaning, leading to less confusion and easy learning and development.

Benefits of Signing with Toddlers

The benefits that both babies and parents get from baby sign language apply to toddlers as well. Many parents of toddlers worry that it might be too late for their little ones to benefit from learning sign language. It isn't. In fact, if your little one has a limited vocabulary, the role sign language will play for his speech development becomes very important.

Like babies, toddlers have their own communication barriers to contend with. Most of them can speak a few words but still find it difficult to express themselves and to talk about their needs and feelings. This can cause your toddler to throw temper tantrums when he cannot easily tell you what's on his mind. In addition, your child may not speak words clearly at first, making it difficult for you to understand what he is saying. For example, your child may use the term "baaa" for ball, bottle, bath, bubbles, etc. If your child uses a sign along with his word "baaa," then you will immediately understand what he's saying and be able to help him pronounce the word more clearly.

Sign language may also be helpful in controlling the emotional tantrums of the "terrible twos" phase. As parents, you'll be able to readily understand your toddler, who will have fewer tantrums and bursts of anger. Any tool that can help to reduce tantrums is a positive advantage to both you and your child.

Teaching sign language becomes even more important when your toddler has not developed speech skills yet. Your child will become increasingly frustrated because he is unable to communicate with you and his language skills are falling behind those of his peers, who are already speaking and using words. By exposing your toddler to sign language, you are giving him a language to use until his speech develops. This will help his social skills in two ways. First, he won't be as frustrated and consumed with trying to communicate with you. This will help his interaction with you and other adults around him because his lack of speech will not become a focus. Second, he won't be as far behind his peers linguistically once he does start talking, making it much easier to be accepted into his peer group.

Benefits of Signing with Toddlers

- Increased vocabulary, leading to better self-expression.
- Elimination of temper tantrums caused by the frustration of not being understood. With the use of ASL your

child will learn how to fill in vocabulary gaps in his communication, making it easier for others to understand what he is trying to say.

- Improvement in social skills as your child becomes confident that he can explain himself to the adults around him. In addition, he won't be as far behind his peers linguistically when his speech does develop.
- Comprehension of language. The toddler years are the best years for your child to learn. Toddlers are little sponges. You will be able to know what your child comprehends and give him more complex language to use.
- Improvement of your toddler's IQ because he is able to use more complex language through the use of signs.
- Linking signs to words to help with language development. When children aren't sure of a word, you can make the sign for them to help trigger the word recognition, which is extremely helpful when learning colors. If the child is unsure of the color, you can sign it to help him remember what the word is for that particular color.

Signing Toddlers

. . . .

Our twins just turned seventeen months today, and I decided to write down how many words they speak out loud and how many they sign. So far, not many words verbally, they do lots of baby talk and maybe six to eight words (dada, mama, and a few others), but they sign over thirty. And I know it would be more if I was more consistent. I remember e-mailing you concerned that they were not signing back. Those days have passed, and now they are little sponges.

What I love about their knowing this language and where we've seen the most benefit is that they tend to calm down when they sign. Toddlers can get frustrated, as you know "help" has been a lifesaver. Lots of time when they are screaming or upset, I ask if they need help, and signing the word calms them down. Also, they have become so polite. "Please" and "thank you" are words they sign frequently. The other day I was at the shoe store, holding Henry, paying for his shoes. We were leaving and I told Henry, "Say 'thank you,'" and he signed it and of course smiled. The clerk was very impressed. They just love to communicate. Sally just today copied me doing the sneeze sign as I was singing the "meatball" song. The "again" sign is so useful as well. When they watch their DVDs, they have favorite parts, and they'll sign 'again' to me so I can rewind and play it again. They like to sign 'again' also when we play or when I sing to them. Finally, something Sally does that just pulls my heartstrings is when her brother falls or is crying, she looks at me with these big eyes and she signs "hurt." Then usually she'll hug him. That gets me every time. I could go on, so many cute stories. I just can't imagine life any different; all parents should do this especially at this age when they aren't talking yet. It's so nice to have that back-and-forth communication; nice for me and I'm sure it is for them as well.

—ANNE B.

Speech Delays and Signing

Children who experience speech delays can benefit greatly from learning sign language. As I discussed earlier, if you give the child signing as a language tool, then you are giving him a meaningful way to communicate with you.

It's interesting how children all develop differently even in the same family. My friend once asked me why her daughter could speak in full sentences and recite numerous songs and stories by heart at the age of two and yet her son at the same age couldn't utter a single intelligible word. She read the same books and sang the same songs with him. Same parents and same parenting—so what made the difference? No one knows for sure why some kids start speaking sooner than others. Even children in the same family will develop at different stages. My son started walking earlier than my daughter, but my daughter started talking earlier than my son. I don't feel I did anything differently with either child. I just think that kids' genetic makeup, even in the same family, is different. Each child is unique and will develop at his own rate and in his own way.

It's important to note that there is a difference between a child who has a speech delay or is a late talker and one who has a language disorder. My son was a late talker—he started saying clear words at around fifteen months—whereas my daughter started talking at eleven months. I wasn't worried because I knew he would catch up once he did start talking. If he was two and not speaking clear words, I would certainly talk to my pediatrician about it. A child who has a language disorder may have difficulty with some of the processing skills that link the brain to the mouth, causing the child to have trouble getting the words out. This requires the help of a speech and language pathologist to teach the child skills that will help alleviate the language disorder.

Most children who are late talkers tend to catch up to their peers with little difficulty once the words start to come. They may need little to no speech therapy. On the other hand, if your child has a language disorder, then he may need the help of a speech and language pathologist. Think of speech delays versus language disorders this way: If you go to start your car and you have a flat tire, you'll have to call someone to get the tire fixed. This flat tire will cause you to leave late for your trip, but once the tire is fixed you can drive there with no problem and reach your destination like everyone else. On the other hand, if you go to start your car and the engine won't turn over because it has a loose wire, then you'll have to get it fixed. The mechanic uses duct tape to fix it and you leave on your trip. A few miles into your trip the duct tape falls off and the car stops again. You go to another garage and have the wire replaced. You start off on your journey and then a storm comes and you hit some ice and skid off into the ditch. You have to wait for a tow truck to get you out. All of these little bumps along the road keep happening and you have to find ways to deal with them in order to get your car to the final destination. The child with a language disorder may never catch up to his peers and may have to work on the disorder well into adulthood. If your child has less than twenty words at eighteen months, you may want to talk to your doctor about having a consultation with a speech and language pathologist. There is a language development chart on my Web site at www.mysmarthands.com. If you visit there you will see more details about speech and language milestones.

Even though it may feel like your child is the only one with a speech delay, it is actually more common than you may realize. Kathryn Ellerbeck, M.D., a pediatrician at the Developmental Disability Center at Kansas University Medical Center in Kansas City, Missouri, states that a surprising 30 percent of children fall in the "outer reaches" of "normal" boundaries. And 10 percent are "abnormally" late in reaching at least one milestone, even though there may be no underlying problem or reason.

Signing and Language Skills

. . . .

My daughter Rosy lost her hearing due to a nearly deadly bout of meningitis when she was thirteen months old. She was an early talker, speaking in sentences before she got sick. Because of the hearing loss, she almost completely lost her ability to talk all together. She is now two and we have started her in speech therapy. She had become so frustrated because she had full sentences in her head that she couldn't access. She would try to talk and actually end up crying, screaming, and even biting her own arms out of frustration. In speech therapy we are teaching her to sign. It's amazing how the physicality of signing the words is allowing her to "tap in" to her language pathways. Using signing has actually made it possible for her to talk. She only has therapy once per week, but she often runs to my laptop and says "baby" and makes her sign for signing at the same time. That means she wants to watch Fireese on YouTube. We don't know anyone else who signs—I took a course in it when I was in high school, but I don't use or remember much of it anymore. I think watch-

ing Fireese has helped Rosy to feel okay and "normal," so she likes it and uses it more. It also has reminded me of signs I already knew, so I can use it more around the house, making it feel more natural for her. So I guess I just wanted to say "thank you."

—BLAKE M.

. . . .

Speech and language pathologist Laura Dyer explains, "It's common to wait until a child is age eighteen to twenty-four months before beginning a formal evaluation of speech and language skills." However, she points to new research on how professionals may be able to "identify at-risk children earlier based on their preverbal behavior." She recommends early intervention with children who have trouble using eye gaze and gestures to make their desires understood. She explains that children who don't babble or use other sounds may be at risk for a language delay:

"Early intervention is important because a child's capacity for learning certain parts of language, which are regulated by brain maturation, is fixed by age three. The first three years are a peak period of development during which the child's brain has twice as many synapses (nerve connections) as an adult's. As a child's brain is stimulated, the synapses are strengthened; if a synapse is used repeatedly in the early years, it becomes permanent. If it is used rarely or not at all, it's unlikely to survive. Children need consistent emotional, physical, cognitive, and language stimulation, starting from birth."

If you feel that your child has a speech delay, you should talk to your pediatrician, who will be able to recommend a course of action for you. Not all children with speech delays have language disorders but all children with language disorders have speech delays. Many late bloomers catch up without any intervention; if you are worried, however, it doesn't hurt to ask.

Sign Language Helps Speech Delays

. . . .

I saw such a difference in my own children—especially my two late talkers—when I started signing with them. My first child was always very frustrated because we couldn't understand him. He would babble in full sentences, and we had no idea what he was saying. We went to a speech pathologist who suggested we use sign language with him. Once we started signing with him we saw a huge reduction in the number of temper tantrums he was throwing. When I had my second child, I started signing with him very early. I saw the amazing benefits it had for my first son, and I wanted to get a jump-start on using it with my second. Signing certainly was a tremendous asset to my children, and I believe it can be a benefit to other children as well—both those who are within the normal range of development as well as those who have communication delays.

—Samantha G.

. . . .

Special Needs and Sign Language

Down Syndrome

Two researchers, Betsy Gibbs and Ann Springer, authors of *Early Use of Total Communication: An Introductory Guide for Parents,* wanted to learn whether sign language combined with speech could help babies and toddlers with Down syndrome and other verbal language delays communicate with others.

They conducted various research projects with children who were able to hear but who were experiencing expressive language delays. Total communication is using any form of communication that is appropriate and may be different at different times. It could be signing, talking, lip reading, finger spelling, writing, and gesturing. The idea is that there isn't just one way of communicating that is beneficial, but all ways can be useful and can be used in combination or at different times. Total communication in Gibbs and Springer's book is used to refer to speaking and signing simultaneously. In their book, they state: "According to the research literature, many young children who have significant delays in language development can benefit from the use of a total communication approach. The method has been particularly useful for children with Down syndrome, autism, apraxia, and other conditions that can cause significant expressive language delays."

The authors point out that sign language is helpful for children with Down syndrome. This is because their comprehension is normally more developed than their expressive speech ability. Signing allows them to show their comprehension of language by using a nonverbal form. The authors give some explanations for why these speech delays may occur and explain how signing can help.

If a child is prone to ear infections and fluid in the ear, it could cause the child to have a hard time hearing words clearly. Their auditory processing (hearing words) may be blurred or muffled, causing them to miss words being spoken. Signing and speaking at the same time aids these children in their understanding of what is being said. They won't miss important words and therefore have an easier time processing language because of the use of signing and speaking at the same time. Additionally, children who have oral motor difficulties (speaking issues) can use signing while they speak so that they could easily be understood. Total communication through the use of both speaking and signing can help tie language together so everyone has an easier time communicating.

Autism

Breaking down communication is one of the most frustrating parts of autism. Kids with autism often struggle with the complexity associated with spoken language. Signing strengthens the development of language and speech. It provides social, emotional, cognitive, and communicative benefits for autistic children, such as:

- Stimulation of speech and language development
  Sign language provides visual stimulation that activates the centers in the brain that are ideally activated by speech. Autistic children tend to excel at visual spatial skills, relating more to pictures than to language. Because signing is very visual and concrete, it can help autistic children with language. For example, the sign "ball" is made by tapping

your fingertips together in the shape of a ball. The sign "ball" looks like a ball. To an autistic child, the sign is more relevant than the word "ball." Sign language provides a bridge between speech and language.

- Reduction of negative social behaviors

    Autistic children often display negative behavior such as anxiety, tantrums, aggression, and self-injury. This behavior worsens if a child does not find a means to communicate his needs and wants. Sign language eases this frustration.

- Increase in social interaction

    Some autistic children have a hard time communicating with words. Signing allows them to respond to people in a way that is comfortable. If your child has nonverbal autism, then signing can play a vital role in their ability to communicate socially.

- Development of cognitive structures

    Sign language complements the development of cognitive structures that are critical for speech and language. It also helps to establish connections in the brain that are critical for encoding language. Encoding language is a necessity when it comes to learning.

Autism and Signing

I wanted to let you know how much you've helped me with my son, Bobby, who is almost four. He is a high-functioning autistic child. Bobby was also born tongue-tied and has a hard time forming everyday sounds. One day I was browsing the Internet, when I came across the video of Fireese at twelve months old doing all these signs. I called Bobby over and together we watched the video several times. He loved it. Within forty-five minutes, my son was able to start communicating with me like never before. I could understand him when he needed a drink, or a diaper change, or his favorite toy (a pink monkey!), or to be left alone. You may not realize this, or believe you're just using your own talents, but you and your beautiful daughter are angels to me. Bobby ended up getting a speech therapist who gave us tons of flash cards with signs on them to learn. He will be four in June, and I'm now looking to find ASL classes to keep up with him. I don't know where we'd be today if we hadn't found your video online—I really don't. Thank you so much for taking the time to put it up and share it. I will always appreciate it.

—IRENE F.

. . . .

Apraxia

Apraxia of speech is a motor-function disorder, which results in difficulty in making movements required for speech. Children suffering from apraxia have the ability to say speech sounds but have a problem with motor planning, which is the planning and execution of a series of movements. You can't get your mouth to do what your brain is thinking and telling it to do.

Imagine the frustration if you know exactly what to say, but when you try to speak, only a fraction of a garbled word comes out—or worse, you say something that does not relate to your thought process. A child suffering from apraxia feels like this.

Although there is no "cure" for apraxia, a child can make a lot of progress with the problems associated with talking. One therapy focuses on the ability to control how fast the child talks. Another focus can be controlling the highs and lows in the voice while talking. In such a focus, rhythm or melody can be helpful. Controlling the rhythm also enables the child to make sentences by putting them together in an easier way.

Sign language is a great tool for children suffering from apraxia. It opens a completely new way for children with apraxia to communicate.

The process of using sign language with children with apraxia is straightforward. The therapist will sign a word ("apple," for example) while saying it. The child is expected to do the same. He would be encouraged to make the sign and say the word aloud. The doubling up of cues helps the child learn and remember a word in two ways. Seeing the sign can provide the child with a visual cue to express a word and slows down the rate of speech. This gives him more time to process what he is trying to say.

Sign language is beneficial to children with apraxia—

• Emotionally:

   It is less frustrating for a child to be able to express what he wants to say at basic levels by signing. Instead of breaking down words and combining incorrect words to form a broken sentence, a child can easily make a sign when he is hungry.

   Coupling voice with signs will help a child to communicate better. Moreover, it provides a positive reinforcement from the parents when the correct sentence is repeated back to him. The child feels less frustrated when he is easily understood, thus resulting in positive communication.

- Socially:

    Children can form a better relation with their peers and adults through the use of sign language. It is difficult for a child to make friends when communicating is a chore. Children with apraxia can often feel excluded from the group and may shy away from socializing or communicating. They can become frustrated and this may lead to social problems. Sign language provides an option for these kids and opens a whole new world of communication to them.

- Academically:

    It is difficult for a child to be academically focused when he is distracted by the pressure to produce speech. Sign language helps a child be more attentive and get involved in the learning process. It can help him to express and construct complete sentences. This will help him to communicate with his teacher effectively.

    Sign language acts as an anchor for children with apraxia. Although sign language cannot replace speech, it is a valuable language tool.

Signing and Apraxia

. . . .

My twenty-eight-month-old daughter, Claire, has a neurological speech disorder called apraxia, and being able to sign has made her very happy. She uses her signs all of the time. I think she's realized that it is so much fun to communicate that it has inspired her and given her confidence to try more. When we started the My Smart Hands class, Claire had about fifteen signs. After only four weeks in the class, she is already up to more than forty signs. She loves to learn new ones and to practice them in class and at home, and I can see that it's really building up her confidence. I can't recommend signing enough, especially for those parents of toddlers and preschoolers who have speech delays or disorders. I tried to find a signing class for more than a year with no luck, and was very excited to see a My Smart Hands class being offered. It has been extremely valuable for us and we look forward to learning more new signs every day.

—JENNIFER H.

3 A Baby's Developmental Milestones

P arents are often curious as to where their child places in relation to a developmental milestone. I remember going to my first few pediatrician's appointments and having her measure my children's weight, height, and head size. I'd always peek over at the chart to make sure they were growing in the way they should. I didn't even realize it at the time, but the doctor was checking that my children were hitting all the correct milestones. Children grow and mature on a curve. Doctors use a standard growth chart developed by the Pediatric Association or Centers for Disease Control to measure a child's development. It is a basic grid from 5 percent to 95 percent and most children, but not all, fall within that grid. If your baby is in the fortieth percentile, it means that 40 percent of boys his age weigh the same as or less than he does and 60 percent weigh more. Your child could be fiftieth for weight but ninetieth for height; the difference between height and weight is fine. If you go to your doctor and your baby falls to tenth for weight when he was once fiftieth, then that's something your doctor might take note of. It doesn't matter if your child starts off at the tenth percentile or the ninetieth, as long as he develops along the curve he started on.

Basically, a developmental milestone is a stage that each child reaches before moving on to the next one. For example, a baby will need to learn to hold her head up before she is able to sit up. She must learn to pull herself up before she can walk. It's good to know what the major milestones are, but don't worry if your child hits them a little later than other children. Remember, children are all different. They each develop at different stages, even within the same family.

My son was a ridiculously early walker—he was only eight months when he started stumbling around. I must say he looked funny walking when his legs barely looked like they could support his body. He crawled for about a month and then got up and started walking. My friend's son, on the other hand, didn't have any interest in walking until he was fifteen months old. He was crawling, sitting, and picking things up, so my friend wasn't worried and she certainly shouldn't have been. Most children will catch up to the others. Now the two boys run and chase each other around; you would never know that one walked so much earlier than the other. Speech is the same way. Children who are late talkers quickly catch up to their peers once the words develop.

I don't think I fully understood what milestones were until I had children. I had a basic understanding, but I wasn't fully aware of each stage and what I should be looking for. In this chapter, we'll look at milestones in some detail and the *approximate* times that children should be hitting those milestones. Your doctor will be looking for any warning signs if your child is not hitting important milestones when she should. If you're concerned at all, don't hesitate to bring it up with him or her.

Before we get into the language milestones themselves, let's talk a bit about how babies learn and understand words.

Understanding Language Learning

Research says that babies start learning words when they are still in the womb. They may not comprehend what is being said, but they pick up on the tones and familiarize themselves with utilizing their auditory channel.

Newborns don't have any conscious awareness of what's going on around them. They only sense; they don't know what they are seeing, tasting, or hearing. For example, when babies eat, they do not even have the knowledge to understand what "eating" is, why they must "eat," or how to "eat." They just have an instinct to cry when they are hungry and to take the food when something is put to their mouths.

After they can focus their eyes, between four and twelve weeks, babies pick up emotions even faster than tones; they sense basic emotions on our faces like love, satisfaction, sadness, and surprise. They subconsciously pick up their parents' body language as well—familiar movements, like caressing and hugging, start developing their own meanings. This is the first step toward comprehension.

As babies grow they continually increase their knowledge of words. They start to understand individual words when they are about four months old. This is the perfect time to focus on key words you feel will be important to them. Emphasize words such as "milk," "mommy," "daddy,'" and "I love you." Signing is a great tool to help emphasize specific words. If you think about it, we don't speak in one-word sentences to our babies. We speak to them in strings of words formed into sentences. If you are asking if a child wants some milk, you may say, "Are you hungry? Would you like some milk?" In that string of words your baby will have to decipher that the important key word is "milk." If you are using signing with the sentence, you will sign the word "milk" and emphasize it a few times by repeating the word while signing it. This allows you to isolate the key word and for your baby to pick up on the subject faster than if you hadn't used a sign. You are simplifying language for your child and making it easier for her to pick it up.

At a very early age babies will start imitating the tongue and lip movements of those around them. The words they hear most often are those they speak first. When you speak, make sure to enunciate the words clearly and don't use abbreviations. A baby's vocabulary list builds up gradually; don't expect your child to speak a new word every other day. To increase the potential rate of learning, teach the words using sign language as well as the spoken word.

Routines are the next step that become clear in a baby's mind; she watches you pour out the cereal, and she knows it's breakfast time. If she sees you getting a book off the bookshelf, she'll prepare herself for a story. If you pick her up and place her beside the bathtub, she'll look at you expectantly to undress her. Babies start "recording" when they see images—they know that when a ball is dropped, it will bounce. They also know that when someone frowns, he's feeling sad. Those reactions indicate that your baby is developing a deeper understanding of actions. It may seem to us that this is naturally developed reasoning, but for a baby, it's not as easy. Many factors contribute to a baby's learning—emotions, colors, movements, and the like. Adding sign language into the learning process makes it easier for babies to link what they are seeing to the word associated with that thing. By simplifying language and by focusing in on the subject through the use of the sign, you are helping your child to understand and learn the important word in that sentence.

Putting Words into Language

At the same time babies are learning words, they are beginning to subconsciously grasp the phrases, tones, and grammar that form a language. You don't teach a baby words without teaching a language at the same time.

I'm sure you've taken a foreign language in school at some point in your life. Do you remember sitting there on the first day of class when the teacher started speaking to you in full sentences and you didn't have a clue what she was talking about? My first foreign language lesson was in French. I thought my head would explode. I had no idea what the teacher was saying, but I could still decipher when one word started and the other finished because of the brief pauses she would make or how her tone changed. Even though I didn't understand the words, I could tell that she was stringing several words together to form sentences. As the year passed and I learned specific French vocabulary, I was able to figure out most of what she was saying by filling in the gaps. I could understand her most of the time based on a combination of the little vocabulary I knew and the tone she used in her sentences. I knew when she was asking a question or making a statement based on the sound of her voice at the end of a sentence. It was helpful having her always speak in French and use words in context.

Think of words and language like this: words are the blocks that make up a language, and language is a house constructed out of those blocks, held together with grammar, syntax, and tone. When a baby is learning a language, she is picking up on the tones and sounds of the sentence you are forming. She may not understand all the words in the sentence, but she is beginning to internalize the language you are using.

When you're teaching your baby a language, it's good to emphasize the key words or subject in a sentence while continuing to use full sentences. For example, if you are asking your baby if she wants "milk," you might say, "Are you hungry? Do you want to have some milk?" Your baby has to decipher what the main topic in that sentence is, milk. Using sign language and signing "milk" at the same time as you say the word and repeating it a few times with the sign helps your child realize what the important word is in that sentence while still using the words in the whole sentence (whole language). This is why signing is so great and helpful to your baby. You can easily continue to use full phrases while highlighting the subject for your child with the use of sign.

Now that we've discussed how babies learn words and language, let's look at developmental milestones.

Developmental Milestones

What Is Child Development?

Every child goes through specific stages of development during her lifetime. Child development involves learning and mastering skills such as sitting, walking, talking, and skipping. Your child will learn these skills with time. There is a developmental milestone for every skill.

What Is a Developmental Milestone?

A developmental milestone is a skill acquired by a child in a specific period. For example, learning how to walk is a developmental milestone. This milestone is generally achieved between the ages of nine and fifteen months.

Milestones develop sequentially, in a stair-step fashion. Normally a baby will need to develop one skill before she can develop the next one. For example, she will need to learn to pull herself up to a standing position before she can attempt to walk. The pulling-up milestone must be met before the child can advance to the walking milestone. Each milestone acquired builds on the last milestone developed.

Your child develops skill in the five critical areas of development:

1. Cognitive development

    This is the ability of your child to learn and solve problems. For instance, your two-month-old baby will learn how to explore the environment with her hands or eyes. Similarly, a five-year-old will learn how to solve simple math problems.

2. Social and emotional development

    This covers the ability of a child to interact with others. For instance, a six-week-old infant will smile at you, a ten-month-old baby will wave his hands, and a five-year-old child will be able to participate in school games.

3. Speech and language development

This is the ability of your child to understand and use speech and comprehend language. For instance, a twelve-month-old baby will be able to say a basic word, a two-year-old will name the body parts, and a five-year-old will learn to say "feet" instead of "foots."

4. Fine-motor-skill development

This refers to your child's ability to use small muscles, particularly hands and fingers. A six-week-old baby might learn to grasp your finger, a two-year-old learns to turn pages one at a time, and a five-year-old learns to master writing letters by holding her pencil correctly.

5. Gross-motor-skill development

This refers to using large muscles. For instance, your six-month-old will learn how to sit with some support, a twelve-month-old baby will pull herself up by holding the furniture, and a five-year-old will learn how to skip.

Speech and Language Development: Newborn to 3 Months

Newborns are very dependent on us for their needs. They need us to feed them when they are hungry, change them when they are dirty, keep them safe and warm, cuddle them, and care for them. Because they are very dependent on us to care for them, they are born with a lovely way of expressing their needs. They do this by crying. In the first three months you and your baby will learn a lot about each other. This is the learning that strengthens the bond between you and provides a foundation for your baby's development. It's also a period that might drive you crazy, trying to figure out what all your baby's sounds mean. This is perfectly normal, and most new parents go through this period of adjustment. By paying close attention to your baby's cries, you will soon realize what different ones mean and how to respond to them.

How your baby uses her hands

- She doesn't have much control over her hands at this age.
- She will open and close her fingers and look at her hand as if it is a foreign object.
- Your baby will start to grab on to your finger if you place it in her hand.

How your baby communicates

- Your baby's cry is her way of communicating her needs.
- Your baby cries to let you know when she is hungry, tired, hot, cold, bored, sick, or wants to be held.
- Your baby may make cooing sounds, "ooh" or "aah" sounds, particularly when you talk to her. Try to make sounds like "ooh," and then pause and see if she'll make the sound back to you.
- Your baby will learn that making sounds is a great way to get attention, and will coo more when you respond.
- Your baby will begin to use different sounds to tell you if she is wet, hungry, tired, or bored. If you listen carefully, you will soon be able to differentiate among these sounds.
- Your baby will use body language to tell you about how she feels. She may try to turn away from you, look in another direction, or begin to cry.

Loving and playing with your baby

- In the first few weeks of life, your baby will sleep much of the time.
- Talking and singing to your baby are the best things you can do to encourage language development. Lullabies introduce your baby to the sound system of language.
- By holding and cuddling your baby often, you are teaching her to trust you.
- Spend a lot of time face-to-face with your baby. You can lay her on your lap and make "ooh" sounds and see if she'll respond to you. Repeat this activity a few times, taking your time to see her reaction.
- Babies are still trying to focus during their first six weeks of life. Make sure to get nice and close to your baby's face, as this will help her to focus on you.
- Smile and talk in a nice, clear voice. Your baby is already familiar with your voice and now she is able to put a face to it.

Child Development: 3 to 6 Months

Your baby is becoming more social. She will smile and laugh as a way to engage you. She will enjoy playing games with you and having books read to her. She will learn how her actions can cause reactions around her. For example, her squealing may make you jump because you are startled or it might make you turn in her direction. She will be gaining better control of her muscles and trying to explore the world around her.

How your baby uses her hands

- Your baby will be able to reach and grab things.
- She can play with her hands.
- She will enjoy reaching her toes.
- She will put all kinds of stuff in her mouth. Be careful to keep small objects that she could choke on out of her reach.

How your baby communicates

- Your baby will imitate more facial expressions.
- She will use different vowel sounds when cooing, oohing, aahing, and making eh-eh-eh-eh sounds.
- She will make more sounds when playing by herself.
- Your baby will squeal, using high- and low-pitched sounds.
- She will growl and gurgle often.
- She will become more active to get attention.
- Your baby will respond differently to a stranger than she will to a familiar person.
- She will smile while looking at herself in the mirror.

Loving and Playing with Your Baby

- Take your baby to different areas of the house to give her different experiences or a change of scenery. This is a perfect time to introduce different signs to your baby. She isn't going to pick up on many signs at this age, but it's a fun way for you to begin practicing your signs.
- Change her position so she can use different parts of her body. You can place her on the floor for tummy time or lay her down face-to-face so she can easily look at you.

- Sing her songs and rhymes, which will get her ready for stories and picture books a little bit later. If you are comfortable, you can start to introduce signs to the songs you are singing. You may want to just start with one sign in the whole song. For example, if you are signing the song "Itsy Bitsy Spider," then you may want to sign "spider" to your child as you sing.
- Once you begin introducing signing, you will find that your child begins to watch your hands as they move.
- Your baby will enjoy playing peekaboo.
- Entertain your baby by giving her pillows, or have her sit on your lap, and give her toys to explore. You can introduce the signs for different toys.
- Read and sign books with bright pictures and use different voices while reading.

Child Development: 6 to 9 Months

At this time, your baby will move into different positions. She will not stay in one place for a long time. She will enjoy playing with toys within her reach. She will find new ways to move toward toys and things that are outside her reach. She will begin to babble and play with sounds, trying to mimic you when you speak.

How your baby uses her hands
- She will be able to grasp the object of her choice in the first few tries.
- She will see tiny things more clearly and will be able to pick them up.

- She will try to hold her bottle or sippy cup.
- She will be able to move a toy from one hand to the other with ease.

How your baby communicates

- Your baby will babble more now than coo. She will blow bubbles and make *b* sounds. She is actually using her speech sounds by utilizing vowels and consonants.
- She will turn her head when you call her name.
- Your baby will start to show signs of favoring toys. She may prefer one stuffed animal to another.
- She may begin to communicate an interest in reading specific books.
- Your baby will begin to communicate a greater sense of independence, wanting more freedom as she begins to explore the world around her.

Loving and playing with your baby

- Talk to your baby whenever you hear her babbling. She will begin to babble back to you, using tones like she is trying to mimic sentences.
- Add more signs to songs you've been singing with her. For the song "Itsy Bitsy Spider," you can add the sign "rain" or "sun."
- Take your baby's hand when you sing a song and see if you can help her sign the words you've been signing to her.
- Sing songs to her and clap her hands along to the beat.
- You can place toys just out of her reach to encourage her to roll over or crawl.

- Hide things under a blanket or box and have her move the object to find the hidden toy.
- Introduce symbolic sounds: the dog says "woof," the car goes "vroom."
- Use real words: "bottle" instead of "baba."

Child Development: 9 to 12 Months

At this point, your baby will be very curious and explore her surroundings. She will be interested in everything. She will be able to roll and turn herself over, and pick up toys or books on her own without your helping her. By the age of one she will say her first word. She will continue to babble and have nonsensical conversations with you. She may babble to herself while playing with toys.

How your baby uses her hands
- Your baby will enjoy picking up and banging toys together.
- She will practice dropping objects and watch them as they go.
- She will learn how to throw things.
- She may want to choose her own foods by feeding herself.
- She will be able to use her thumb and index finger to pick up small objects.
- She will like to put items into buckets or fit toys that are shapes into specific holes.

How your baby communicates
- Your baby will use her pointer finger to show something that interests her and to share it with you. She will learn to look at things you point to as well.

- When you say no, she will stop what she is doing and may look at you.
- Your baby may understand no, but may not obey. This is normal development.
- She will recognize familiar words such as "bye-bye."
- She may try to imitate the things you do.
- She may say her first word during this time and will know what it means.

Loving and playing with your baby

- Whenever your baby points at something, name it for her. Repeat the name and encourage her to try to say the word.
- Make a safe place where she can crawl and play. This allows her to explore the world and show you what her interests are. You can pick specific things she is interested in and show her the sign for those things.
- When reading a book, focus on one object on the page and sign the word you are focusing on. Take her hands and help her make the sign for the word.
- Encourage her to make a sign for something she is interested in. If you know she wants a ball, don't simply give her a ball; instead, ask her if she wants the ball while signing "ball." Help her to sign "ball," and then give it to her.
- When singing her songs, you can pause to see if she'll say the word that comes next in the song. You might sing, "The itsy bitsy _____" and see if she'll say "spider." You can sign "spider" as you pause to help give her a clue of what word comes next.

- Narrate your day. If you are getting ready to go out, you can say, "Mommy is putting on her black coat." Use descriptive language.

Child Development: 1 to 2 Years

How to walk and talk are the biggest challenges for your child during this time. She will want to become more independent as she learns how to walk but may not have the coordination. Her speech and language skills also have rapid growth during this time. She will realize words have meanings. Your baby will learn how to communicate her needs and feelings. She will begin to use two syllables together, like "baba" for "bottle." During this stage she will understand simple requests like "Get your shoes." Her comprehension of language will develop very quickly during this stage.

How your child uses her hands
- Your baby will try to use a spoon or fork instead of finger feeding.
- She will enjoy using crayons.
- She will like stacking things up and then knocking them down.
- Your baby will enjoy nesting cups and toys that fit on top of each other.
- She will enjoy shape sorters or puzzles.
- Your baby will try to take things apart.
- She will enjoy exploring kitchen cupboards and will pull things out and try to put them back in.

How your child communicates

- Your baby is slowly learning how to communicate her needs and feelings by the means of words and expressions.
- She will point at images or her body parts. Teach her the words and signs for the things she is pointing at.
- Your baby will say words that are familiar to her surroundings. She will know at least fifty words by the age of twenty-four months.
- She may pronounce things incorrectly, saying "ba" instead of "ball."
- Your baby will join two or three words together by her second birthday.
- "No" will be a well-used word by your child. Your baby may often say "no" when she means "yes."

Loving and playing with your child

- Make sure that you make dressing and undressing a fun experience for your child. You can play a game where you lay out the clothes and then sign an item and see if your child can pick out the item you are signing.
- Expect tantrums at this age as your child will wish to explore things and often get frustrated when you try to limit this exploration. Teaching the sign "help" can be useful. By giving your child the tool to easily ask for help, she will feel more confident exploring her surroundings.
- Read and sign books that are repetitive and rhyme. Your child will love rhyming beats.
- Play "show me" with books and ask your baby to point and show you things/objects. Teach your child the signs for those items as well.

- Identify colors in books or using toys you are playing with.
- Use descriptive language when playing with her: "black cat," "red car." Help her begin to use descriptive language. If she says, "car," you say, "What color is the car? The car is red."

Growth will be rapid for your child during the first two years. She will experience a lot of milestones in a short period of time. Everything is a new learning experience. Each new task learned will be a challenge in and of itself. The best thing you can do for your child during this period is talk to her. Read her books, narrate your day, and talk to her about what she is doing when she plays with toys or eats her meal. She will learn the most from you during this period. Adding signs allows you to highlight key words and simplify language while still introducing her to full sentences. By signing and talking with your child at the same time, you are giving her two ways to communicate with you. Signing allows her to use a language before her words develop. By giving her a language-rich environment, you are creating a great foundation for her. How your child develops in such a short period of time is absolutely fascinating. You will be excited and amazed and so proud as she progresses through each stage!

Part II

Laura's Step-by-Step Guide

Step 1: Good to Go? Recognizing Readiness

This book will be your guide and resource as you begin your signing journey with your baby. You'll find suggestions of which words to start with, what games to play, and how to use signing in other circumstances. You can easily flip to the back of the book and look up a word. Learn that word and teach it to your baby. When you are ready, you can add another word to your signing repertoire. Before you know it, you'll have a handful of signs.

When to Start Signing

When is the right time to begin signing? There is never a "perfect" time. Experts recommend starting between four and eight months, but it is never too early or too late.

You can start signing to your baby as early as you like; we talk to our babies as soon as they are born, and we can do the same with signing. Just because a child doesn't yet respond verbally or with gestures doesn't mean he doesn't understand what's going on. Most babies have heard words spoken to them for at least a year before they actually start saying words. On the other hand, if your little one is older and you want to sign with him, there will still be huge benefits to doing so. You don't have to worry that you've waited too long and missed the boat. Signing is beneficial to children of all ages.

The decision as to when to start signing is completely up to you. There are, however, a few things you'll want to assess to help you determine if you are ready to begin. It really depends on your personality. If you're the type of person who likes to have immediate gratification, I would suggest starting when your baby is around six to eight months old. However, if you're the type who's really dedicated and will continue to sign for months until your baby eventually signs back, go ahead and start as early as two to four months.

Recognizing Your Child's Readiness

Your baby will need to observe you doing the signs for several months before she comprehends that the signs you are making mean something. Your baby will comprehend the signs before she is able to do them herself. It's like learning any other language; you have to hear (or see) the words several times before you are able to lock them into your memory. When many parents first begin to learn how to sign, it doesn't always come naturally to them. Because you're learning a new language at the same time, it might feel a little funny signing to your baby at first. This repetition stage of signing will help you get into a nice routine of reminding yourself to make the signs when you say the words.

You can observe your child for signs that he is ready and interested in communicating. This may include eye gaze or a sound to get your attention, or natural gestures such as pointing or reaching for something. Your child may point to or make an animal sound for his favorite animal book. He may reach for a glass to show that he is thirsty. All of these actions indicate a readiness for the introduction of sign language. I had a friend who didn't start signing consistently with her babies as early as she could have, but when her babies started using gestures of their own, she realized, "Hey— we need to start signing!"

She once said to me, "I suspect my children would have started signing earlier if I had introduced them to signs around six months rather than waiting until they were closer to a year old, but again each child has his or her own timetable for learning and I started signing when I first noticed them using gestures and demonstrating a desire to communicate."

At the end of the day, parents should remember that each child is unique and has a different speed of progressing. And nobody knows when your child is ready to start learning baby sign language better than you do, because no one knows your baby better than you do.

Never Too Late

If your child is already talking, you may think that there's no point in introducing sign language. The reality is that it's never too late to benefit from signing with your children. My daughter was a very early talker and had a fairly large vocabulary very quickly, but signing was still beneficial for her. I found that many of the words she learned were the ones she first signed. As I mentioned earlier, toddlers can become very frustrated if they aren't being understood. I remember when my mother was babysitting and my daughter was standing at the fridge and asking her for something. She stood there and said, "I want 'dodo,' please." My mom told her she didn't understand what "dodo" was. Fireese said it again while she was trying to find it in the fridge. She was pulling things out and getting more and more frustrated with her grandmother. She began throwing things on the floor and crying. My mom said to her, "Do you know the sign for what you want?" Fireese turned to her and signed "avocado" very clearly. My mom knew that sign, as Fireese had been using it for quite some time. Grandma had never heard her say the word "avocado" and didn't realize "dodo" meant "avocado." Thankfully, Fireese was able to use a sign even though she could say a good approximation of what the word was.

Recognizing Your Readiness

Just as it is important for your child to be ready, it is equally important that you are ready. Some parents are apprehensive about signing with their babies when they don't know the language themselves. How can you teach your baby something that you don't know? I realize this can be intimidating, but it's nothing to be concerned about. Because you are not teaching the full grammar and syntax of the language, you can easily learn as your baby does. Just pick a word to begin teaching your little one, look up that sign, and start using it. It's that simple. For example, if you want to teach your child the sign for milk but you don't know the sign, just go look it up. If you forget the sign, you can look it up again in a second. Then, when you're ready for the next sign, you simply look that one up and introduce it. Before you know it, you will have a long list of signs that you've learned and can teach to your baby.

The first few months of having a new baby can be overwhelming. You're trying to get into a nice routine of feeding and sleeping, just for starters. You have this new person in your life and he's with you 24/7. It's definitely an adjustment. You may not want to introduce something new until you've established a basic routine with your baby and are comfortable with it.

You'll know when you're ready when you feel like you've established a nice routine and have gotten to know your little one. I knew my children were ready when I could hold their gaze. My daughter would look at my face as if she were studying me. She seemed to pay attention to what I was doing. If I pointed at something, she would look from my face to my hands. I knew *I* was ready when I was getting bored with reading the same books over and over and playing the same games. It was a perfect time for me to introduce signing because it added an extra fun element to our day.

Starting and Stopping

Some parents start signing with their babies and then, for whatever reason, they stop. If you've tried signing and stopped because you felt you couldn't do it, then you're not alone. Don't get discouraged; it just means you weren't ready yet. This happens all the time. Some start too early and then give up, but you can always start again. Maybe they hadn't established a good routine yet, and adding one more thing to a new life with baby was too much.

Some parents stop signing when they travel with their baby. Everything is disrupted while away from home. Sleep is different, eating can change, and routine in general gets flipped on its head. You may find signing while on vacation easy to remember, and that's great, but on the other hand, you may forget to sign, especially if you're new to it and still trying to establish a signing routine. If you do drop the signing while on vacation, simply pick it up again once you get back home. Just don't expect to fall back into an instant routine. Your may need to reestablish sleep patterns and other important things all over again. Take your time and get the basics under control before adding the signing back in. If your signing expectations are too high, then you may feel discouraged.

Sometimes a parent drops signing because of illness. It's hard taking care of baby and yourself when you aren't feeling well. You're likely to forget a lot of things during this time just in order to do the bare minimum. It's okay if you don't sign during this time; cut yourself some slack. We're all human and can only do so much. When you feel better and are back to your old self, then try to incorporate signing again. You may even have to go back to square one with the signs. This is completely normal. If you're aware that it's okay to stop and start, then you will have a greater chance of being successful in the future.

Take comfort in the fact that it's completely normal for parents to start signing before they are ready or to experience bumps in the road once they have started. Instead of giving up totally, just give yourself some time and then try again.

It's Never Too Late!

. . . .

I was a teacher before I had my son, Liam. I always knew that I wanted to sign with my baby when I had one. I was so excited when he came that I started signing right away. I was really committed to it. Then I developed colitis and became very sick. I could barely take care of myself, let alone my baby. It took several months to get the colitis under control and feel back to normal. During that time my husband had to pick up the slack around the house. He did most of the cooking and cleaning. My primary job was to feed and cuddle Liam. Signing went by the wayside. By the time I felt better he was almost eleven months old. I figured there was no point at this age, as he was starting to develop a few words. Then one day he was watching Sesame Street *and they were using sign language on it. Later that night we were reading a story and he signed "dog" in the book. I was amazed! He picked up the one sign from just watching a show for the five minutes I had it on. I then picked up signing with him again and he ate it up. He learned new signs fairly quickly. Over the next year and a half the signs came in handy (pardon the pun). I would definitely tell parents it's never too late to sign with your baby, and if you stop for whatever reason, do consider picking it up again.*

—TAMMY N.

. . . .

Points to Remember

- The perfect time to begin signing with your baby depends on you and your child. It is never too early or too late to benefit from sign language.
- Is your baby ready? Does he hold your gaze for a few seconds? Does he look at your hands when you move them around or point at things? Does he wave bye-bye? All of these things are signs that your baby may be ready to learn signs.
- Are you ready? Just as your baby has to be ready, you must be as well. Do you have a good routine set up for your child? Do you find you are looking for more activities to do with your baby throughout the day? Are you confident that you can take on a new activity without feeling overwhelmed? If you answered yes to these questions, then you're probably ready to start signing with your baby.
- Don't worry if you start signing and then stop. Give yourself a few weeks and try again. Don't give up fully. Just know it wasn't the right time to start.
- Be confident in yourself and your baby. You will both be able to learn to communicate through the use of sign language with the help of this book.

Step 2:
Milk, More, Eat.
Getting Started

Now that you've decided *when* to begin signing, the big question is *how*.

When introducing ASL to your child, I'd encourage you to start with one to five signs. This is not for the baby's sake, but rather for yours. If you're not used to signing, it may be hard for you to remember to do it throughout your day. If you pick just one sign at first, you'll have a better chance of remembering to do that sign. The key to successful signing is consistency. Whenever you say the word, make the sign. Your baby will learn the signs faster if you show the sign every time you say the word. It is more important to sign one word consistently than several words sporadically throughout your week. If you are consistent, it will be clearer to your baby that your action (the sign) means the same thing as the word you are saying. If you aren't consistent, you won't be as successful.

The First Signs

So how do you choose the first signs? A great one to start with is "milk." Think about it: your baby's life is filled with sleep (which they often fight), milk (which they love), and poop (do you really want this to be your baby's first sign?). A thing that they love and that dominates their day, such as milk, is the most logical choice for the first word to teach.

What other words should you add in? Child psychologists have learned that toddlers typically understand six basic concepts and can use them very early in their communication. The following list will help you identify the concepts your infant understands and the types of things for which she may want to learn signs.

1. Naming something (milk, dog, book)
2. Addressing someone (Daddy, Mommy, Grandma)
3. Finding something (Where's the shoe? Where's the cat?)
4. Noticing that something is gone (no toy, food all gone)
5. Asking for more (more milk, hide again)
6. Possessing something (my bear, your sock)

Initially, everyday simple activities and needs such as eating, drinking, or changing diapers are perfect opportunities to introduce signs. I suggest you start with the signs "milk," "more," and "eat," which are among the simplest to make. You may want to stick to these basic signs until your infant starts making them. Then you can add more signs to your daily routine as your baby catches on to the fun and satisfaction signing brings. Be sure to start with a couple of signs that *you* are comfortable teaching. Some additional first sign suggestions are "finished," "water," "mom," "dad," "dog," "cat," "diaper," and "bath." The older your child is, the faster he will pick up signs. With both of my children, signing exploded after their first birthdays. I would show them a sign for something once and they'd pick it up. They also became interested in learning new signs. They would grab a book and point to a picture, asking for the sign. At a certain point, they grasped what we already knew: that this was a wonderful form of communication that gave Mommy, Daddy, and other adults around them a much greater understanding of their needs.

The Five Phases of Signing

While all babies take to signing in different ways, the general process is fairly consistent and can be broken down into five phases.

Phase 1: Observing and babbling

At first, it's likely that your baby will simply watch as you make signs. When my daughter, Fireese, was four months old, she loved watching and playing with my hands as I'd sign "milk" during nursing. It was as though she was trying to figure out what I was doing but hadn't yet made the connection. Your baby may also begin to babble with her hands just like she will with words. She may wave them around and open and close them and look to you for some reciprocal communication.

Phase 2: Realizing that signs have meaning

It may happen gradually or all at once, but your child will soon realize that the gestures you have been doing with your hands actually mean something. It wasn't long before my daughter figured out that the hand motion I was making before nursing time was the sign for milk. When she saw the sign, she'd get very excited—waving her hands and kicking her feet. She knew what was coming. It was 100 percent clear that she understood what that sign meant. She still wasn't producing the sign, but it was fun knowing that she understood it.

A child may need to see a sign many different times in several different contexts before he understands what the sign means. For example, the first few times you teach the word "book," you may grab your child's favorite book and sign the word. The child may not realize that sign has anything to do with reading a book. He may simply be so looking forward to reading that he didn't make the connection. The next time you sign the word "book," he may think that you are talking about that particular book you are reading and not "book" as an object. After several times using the sign with different books in different settings, your baby will realize that the common denominator is a book and that sign must mean "book."

Once your child learns the connection between the sign and the thing it represents, he may start asking you in a nonverbal way for more signs. For example, when I sat and read books with my daughter, I would ask her to show me the signs in the book. If we came across a word she didn't know the sign for, she would point at it and look at me to show her the sign. It's wonderful when they make the connection that everything has a sign and they want to learn those signs so they can communicate with you. It's amazing to see what they are thinking, and signing allows you a window into their little minds.

Phase 3: Imitating signs

Eventually, your baby will probably try to copy the signs you do. When my daughter first started using the signs "more" and "finished," it was in response to my questions, "Do you want 'more'?" and "Are you 'finished'?" I modeled the signs for her as I said them, and she was then able to respond accordingly.

Don't worry if your child doesn't imitate. Some children learn a sign strictly through observation. You may have signed "shoes" to her several times without her ever copying it. Then one day you may be getting her dressed and she'll surprise you by suddenly signing "shoes."

Bath Time Routine
. . . .

When my daughter, Claire, was ten months old, we used to have a bedtime routine into which we'd incorporate sign language. We would do bath, and I would sign "bath." Then we'd get changed into her pajamas, and I would sign "pajamas." Then came story time, and I would sign "book." Next was bed, and I would sign "sleep." I had been signing this bedtime routine with Claire for a number of months, but she hadn't yet signed anything back to me except for "book." One day my husband and I were out with friends and got home late. We decided to skip bath time and just put Claire in her pajamas and read her a story. As I was reading to her, she was fussing and seemed very upset. I figured she was overtired and I tried to put her in her crib. As I laid her down, she looked up at me and signed "bath." This was the first time she had made that sign since I started teaching her. I was amazed! I guess there was no reason for her to have made the sign before now. It was a wonder that she was able to tell me she was upset because I had missed a part of her bedtime routine, something that was clearly very soothing to her. If it weren't for sign language, I would have just assumed she was overtired. This was a great communication moment for us.

—BETH R.

. . . .

Sometimes, imitation can happen in strange ways. When my son, Hartford, was a baby, he did a very cute thing. Whenever I'd ask him if he wanted more of something, he would take my hands and tap them together. He didn't understand that he could make the sign with his own hands; he thought he had to use mine. It was adorable having his tiny little hands try to tap my two hands together to show me that he did want more.

Many parents don't realize their child is signing until the child consistently does that motion a few times. Parents are looking for their child to sign the word the way they do and may miss the approximation of the sign that the baby is actually doing. For example, many babies will clap their hands for "more" or they will tap their index fingers to their palms. They haven't mastered the proper way to sign "more," but they are trying. It's the same for speech. Your baby isn't going to pronounce words properly at first. They may say "baaa" for "bath" or "daa" for "dog." Eventually their language matures into the correct pronunciation.

Phase 4: Using signs to communicate

Once your child knows what signs mean and has imitated several signs, he will be ready for the next step: signing independently to tell you what is on his mind. This is the fun part. You will find that your child has so much to tell you. He may point to a dog and use the sign for dog, or you may find that he notices the beautiful flowers as he signs "flowers."

Our children notice so many things that we often overlook. For example, my son may make the sign for fish. I wonder what he is talking about, since I don't see a fish anywhere. Then I notice it—a little stuffed animal, or a picture, or a print on someone's T-shirt, and I am able to exclaim, "You're right—there is a little fish in that picture, isn't there?" As a parent, you get such a great feeling knowing what your child is thinking and being able to acknowledge that. And it's wonderful for a child to be able to communicate his thoughts and have Mommy or Daddy respond with ease.

Signing Enhances Outdoor Time

I am so glad that my son knows sign language. We were out for a walk yesterday and we were singing songs and talking about all the fun things we were seeing on our walk. My son just loves fire trucks. When I heard one coming, I noticed he was getting excited, so I began talking about the red fire truck. Then I noticed him signing "dog" over and over again. I looked around and saw a huge Great Dane in the park, chasing a Frisbee. My son had no idea that a fire truck was even coming. He was fixated on this huge dog running after a Frisbee. I was so glad he had sign language to tell me what he was thinking. That way I could change my conversation to what interested him. I always tell people that signing with him gives me a window into his thoughts and that I can talk to him about things that are relevant to him.

—Natasha T.

Phase 5: Pairing signs and speech

Many signs will probably come before speech, but some words and sounds may come first or at the same time as the signs. My son, Hartford, learned his animal signs at the same time he learned animal sounds.

He still can't say the words for "snake" or "horse" or "rabbit," but he vocalizes "sssss" as he makes the sign for snake, "neigh" as he makes the sign for horse, and "hop hop hop" as he signs "bunny."

Hartford came to me one day and said, "Baaa," his voice filled with excitement. "What?" I asked. "You want to play ball?" Again he said "baaa," this time in a frustrated tone. I asked him to show me the sign for what he wanted. He did the sign for bath. "Do you want a bath?" I asked. He took off running down the hall toward the bathroom—it turned out that his sister was running the water in the sink and he thought it was time to have a bath. He loves his bath. I was so glad that he was able to clearly tell me what he was thinking and that I didn't have to sit and play a guessing game with him.

When Hartford was sixteen months he started to vocalize more and more, but many of his words were still difficult to understand. By pairing the spoken word with a sign, we could understand him much more clearly than if he just used one or the other.

Many of my daughter's utterances started out as word approximations paired with a sign. The word became clearer until we were able to understand the word without the sign. When some of her words became clear enough to be understood without the sign, she would naturally drop those signs.

When teaching both verbal language and sign language, it is important to model correct speech or signs for your child. When your child starts saying "baaa" for "ball," you will want to continue calling the ball by its proper name and not by the approximation your child is saying. This will help your child to say the word correctly faster, versus using the "baaa" term your child is starting to use.

This is the same with sign language. Many babies will use sign approximations. For example, my daughter used to sign "water" with her whole flat hand on her mouth rather than tapping the letter *w*. Making the letter *w* is hard for little fingers. I continued to sign it the right way, however. I did this for two reasons: first, if I started signing the way that she did, then she would be seeing me use a different sign and would be confused; second, I want her to eventually learn how to do the sign the right way.

Likewise, if a child says in English, "Her likes ice cream," an appropriate response would be to agree with the statement while modeling the correct response: "Yes, you are right—she does like ice cream, doesn't she?" It could be discouraging for a child if you focus on what he said incorrectly, such as, "No, honey, she likes ice cream, *not* her likes ice cream."

Five Tips for a Successful Beginning

Now that you've figured out what signs you'd like to start with, and have familiarized yourself with the phases of signing, you're ready to begin. As you start your signing journey, keep the following tips in mind. They'll help you get off to a great start.

1. Consistency and repetition

When signing with your baby, consistency is more important than anything else. When parents first start signing with their children, it may not feel natural. Parents in my classes sometimes report that they feel silly signing. This is because it isn't your first language and you are learning along with your infant. You aren't yet in the habit of signing and therefore it feels awkward. This is totally natural.

It's like when you first buy a new pair of jeans, they feel stiff and uncomfortable and all you want to do is put on your old jeans again because they fit you so well. But you know that in time they will be just as comfortable on you as your old ones were, once you work them in. This is the same as learning to sign. You need to break in the language before it feels completely comfortable to you.

If you think about it, a new language is much easier to pick up if words are being introduced in context as well as being introduced frequently. This is the same for a baby learning the signs. Let's say you start signing ten words to your infant but you only remember to sign them occasionally when you say the word. This will make it more difficult for your child to link the word with the sign. If you say the word "milk" ten times a day and only sign it twice, then your baby won't pick up the sign as quickly as if you signed the word ten times.

Just before you begin feeding, ask your baby, "Do you want milk?" Emphasize the word "milk" while making the sign. If you are nursing, you can ask the question as you begin your prenursing routine. If you are bottle-feeding, prepare the bottle first, hold it up near your face, and ask your baby the question while signing "milk" near the bottle. You can also sign "milk" while your baby is feeding, to reinforce the idea.

I love teaching baby-signing classes because it's an opportunity for me to help guide parents who don't have any signing experience at all to the point where their child signs back to them and wants to learn more signs. I once had a mom take my class who by week five was disappointed that her daughter wasn't signing to her yet. Her daughter was eleven months old and should have picked up at least one sign in the five weeks since the class had begun. I asked the mom about her routine and how she used signing during the day. She said that she made sure to sign at least one word a day, introducing new ones each day. I asked her if she had any signs that she consistently used throughout her day. She said, "I try, but not always." This is a common thing I hear from parents when they are frustrated that their child hasn't signed back to them. I told this woman to go home and only sign one word all week, picking a word that is used frequently and that her daughter likes. She chose the sign for cracker because her daughter loved little teething biscuits, which she, the mom, called crackers. The woman came to class the following week and said that it worked. Her daughter now signs "cracker" each and every time she wants one. And her baby was now picking up signs very quickly. It was like a light bulb had gone on in the child's head when she realized that her mom was showing her the signs that went along with certain words.

If you take away only one thing from this book, then this is it: consistency is the key.

2. Take your child's hand and show her how it feels to make the sign

While your baby is having milk, you can gently take her hand. Open and close it while saying, "Yes! That's right, you are having milk."

If you are signing "more," you can take your baby's hands and show her how it feels to make the sign. Then respond to the sign by giving her more of what she is having. By making the response to the sign immediate, your baby will understand that that action will get results, in this case more of what she is eating.

Many babies can recognize the parent doing the sign but don't realize they can make the sign. When my children would nurse, I would take their hands and open and close them, saying, "Yes! You're having milk! Milk! This is the sign for 'milk.'" I would also take their hands and tap them together and say very excitedly, "More, you want more? Sure, here is 'more.'" And I would really emphasize the word "more" while helping my children make the sign. Your baby may laugh at you when you first start doing this, but that is okay; she'll eventually realize she can do that without your help and get a response from you as well.

3. Don't anticipate and respond immediately to your child's needs

Don't overthink your child's needs when you are teaching her to sign. This is easy for us to do as parents, but your child will learn to sign faster if you try to ask her for a sign versus simply giving her what she wants. You may know that your baby wants milk, but you don't have to respond to her immediately. If you do, there is no reason for your baby to sign. Play dumb! Ask, "What would you like? Would you like some milk?," really emphasizing the word "milk." Then you can take your baby's hand and help her sign "milk," saying at the same time, "Milk? You want milk? Sure, here is 'milk.'" And then give her the milk. This will show her that she can make the sign to get the item she wants. Of course you'll want to give your child what she wants after you've asked for the sign, because you don't want her to become frustrated. You just want to tenderly encourage the sign.

If you know your child wants more of something, you can ask, "Do you want 'more'?" and make the sign "more" as you say the word. Then give her more of whatever she is having. By taking your time and not overthinking your child's needs, you are encouraging her to use her signs. In a situation like this you know what she wants, so you can help her make the right sign for the situation. Eventually, she will realize that if she makes that sign she will get the item.

4. Make it fun and look for teachable moments

Signing shouldn't be a chore but, rather, fun. Don't worry about carving out time in your day to sit your child down to teach signing. There's no need. Signing can be used throughout your day in a natural way by incorporating it smoothly into your routines. If your child is crying because she is hungry and you know she wants milk, make the sign "milk." If this action seems to irritate her for some reason—maybe she's really hungry or tired—simply give her the milk. The purpose of signing is to *reduce* frustration for both you and your baby, not to add to it. Even though I do recommend being consistent, there are times when you may not be able to teach the sign the way you would like. That is perfectly fine. Remember, signing should be fun for both of you. If it's not enjoyable at that moment, then simply move on. Eventually, your baby will recognize the sign, which will bring about a happy feeling because she knows what is coming.

Motivational signs are things that your baby is interested in or likes. For example, if your child hates apples, there's no point working on the sign "apple" because there's no motivation to learn that sign. On the other hand, if your little one loves bananas, then she will be motivated to learn that sign. You will eventually be able to introduce all sorts of signs, but you will definitely want to begin with signs that will be motivating to your baby.

Motivational Food Signs

When signing with your baby, it's a good idea to look for things your baby likes and show her the sign for that particular object; your baby will be more motivated to learn how to make those signs. When teaching your baby food signs, you will want to start with a food that she really loves. If your child loves Cheerios, then teach her the sign for Cheerios. Your baby will be more interested in learning that sign than a sign for a food that she dislikes.

When introducing food signs, ask your baby if she wants to eat before you begin feeding her. Make the sign "eat." Then you can say, "Do you want Cheerios?" and show her the sign for Cheerios (we sign the letter o for Cheerios because we called them o's, but you can sign "cereal" if you like). You can even take your baby's hand and show her how it feels to make the sign. If your baby doesn't seem interested in the sign, don't worry; you'd be surprised at how much they pick up in their peripheral vision. You can teach as many food signs as you like; it's up to you how many. But try to include at least one new sign during mealtimes every few weeks.

When teaching your child sign language, you can also look for teachable moments. You will have the regular signs that you're working on with your baby, and are consistent with, but you may want to introduce motivational signs during teachable moments. For example, if your child is playing with cars and seems to be showing a huge interest in them, you may want to take this opportunity to show him the sign for cars. It's okay to teach new signs throughout your day that you may not sign consistently as long as you have signs that you use regularly. And who knows, maybe he'll pick up the motivational sign you showed him before any others. Just consider these signs bonus words until you are ready to put them into your regular arsenal.

5. Don't be too hard on yourself

At first, many parents find it hard to remember to sign throughout the day. It might even take you a few weeks to get into the routine of signing. That's perfectly natural. Don't let that make you feel as if you can't do it—all parents go through a learning curve with signing. The key is to not give up. Everyone can do it. Once your baby signs back to you, it will become much easier to keep up with the signing and introduce new signs. So cut yourself some slack if it takes a while to fall into a signing routine. You will get there.

Remember, you are learning a new language too. Because it doesn't come as second nature to you, like speaking does, it will take some time for you to remember to be consistent. This is totally fine. Just because consistency is the key doesn't mean that you can't have a learning curve getting to the consistent point. This is one of the hardest things when you first start learning to sign with your baby. I've had many parents report that it's hard to remember to sign throughout their day. I always say it is fine; if you forget a few times, you will eventually get better at remembering and it will feel more comfortable in no time.

The important thing is to stay with it. For me, as an educator, there is nothing more frustrating than hearing a parent say, "I tried signing with my baby, but it just didn't work." I have never heard of a baby who didn't sign if her parent signed consistently with her and didn't give up. You have to remember that your baby doesn't say any words to you for several months after being born. Does this mean you don't talk to her until she is ready to talk back to you? No! You continue to introduce words and language to her by speaking, reading, and signing. Just like any other language, if a baby is exposed to signing she will pick it up eventually.

I also hear parents say, "It was too hard for me to remember to sign." I understand this fully. When I first started signing with my daughter, I had a hard time remembering to do it. I had a background in sign language but had never used it at home, so it was a new thing that I added to my home routine. I did forget to sign a lot in the beginning. However, I had done enough research on signing with babies that I knew it would work, so I was motivated to continue.

I found when I viewed signing as an extension of other activities, it was much easier to remember to include it in my day. Being on maternity leave was sometimes hard because it meant long days of being alone with my baby and having to be the "entertainer." I would narrate my day to her, read books, play games, and talk about the activities we were doing. By using sign language, I had a wonderful opportunity to enhance all those activities. When I read a book with my daughter, it would take longer when I used signs along with reading the book. All of a sudden, my long days were filled with this additional activity that was very easy to incorporate and made our activities much more fun.

If you start with only one word, then it won't be difficult at all. Don't overwhelm yourself with too much at first. You'll find that once your baby starts signing back to you, you will be motivated to continue to sign and introduce more words to her.

Step 3: More Cheese. Branching Out

When will my baby start signing back to me? How long will it take for him to pick up signs? I get these questions from parents all the time. Unfortunately, there is no magic answer. Signing is much like talking: you never know when a child is going to start talking; they just do it when they are ready. As I mentioned previously, I signed with both my children when they were four months old, and my son started signing when he was six months and my daughter not until she was almost ten months. My daughter started talking early, and my son was a little later with his words. All children are different. If you put into practice all of the tips I have given in this book, then you will have the greatest chance of being successful.

You as the Teacher

As your child's teacher, you will require a lot of patience. You will need to learn how to wait. We don't expect our babies to copy our words when we first start speaking to them. We wait and see when

they are ready to begin speaking and then we focus on emphasizing certain words. The same goes with signing. You can begin to
introduce signs to your baby, but have patience and know they
won't necessarily sign back right away.

Babies will take weeks or months to make their first sign. This is
because they first need to learn how to associate the gesture with
the word. Just as teachers in a classroom need to get to know each
child and their learning styles, you will need to assess the same
thing with your baby. I found that with my daughter I had the
most success teaching her signs when she was sitting in her high
chair. She was incredibly patient and focused on me during mealtimes. She could sit there for hours as we chatted, sang, read stories, and ate our meals. This situation was ideal for teaching her
signs, as we had great face-to-face time. My son, on the other hand,
would not sit in his high chair for any length of time. It was always
a battle to get him to sit and focus on eating, let alone anything
else. I had to make sure the food was ready before I put him in the
high chair and then it was a quick feed and down again. This situation was not an ideal teaching time for him. If I tried to sign with
him during mealtimes, it would have been pointless and driven
both of us crazy. Instead, he was very focused when playing on the
floor. We often had snack time on the floor as he would sit and
happily eat his food and look at me. These were great times to introduce signs. What worked for one child did not work for another.
You need to assess what will work best for your child when it comes
to introducing signs.

Watch for Approximations

In the last chapter, we talked about word approximations—the way that babies often use sounds (like "baaa" for "bath") in place of specific words. The same is true for signing. In the beginning, your child will not always produce a perfect sign. But watch the actions your child is making with his hands. I once had a mom whose baby was signing "more" for the longest time before the mom realized it. The baby was in my class and I could see him trying to sign "more" by clapping his hands together instead of squeezing the tips of his fingers and thumbs together and then tapping his hands against each other. I said to the mom, "Oh great! Charlie is signing 'more'!" She was shocked, as she had no idea that clapping was his way of signing the word. He was so excited when his mom finally "got it." So make sure to watch your baby carefully for sign approximations. Both my children would tap their index finger on their forehead for the sign "daddy." They didn't hold their hands open and tap their thumb, but I still knew what they were trying to sign. If you don't watch for efforts like this, you might miss your child's first attempts at signing.

This is an important point when signing with your baby: if you realize that your child is doing a sign approximation for a word, *don't change the way you sign the word to match his way of signing it.* This will confuse your baby. If your baby claps his hands for the sign "more," don't start clapping your hands. Keep signing the same way you always have. If you change to match your baby's way, he will no longer recognize the sign. This will be confusing for your child. In the same way that you still say words correctly, saying "bottle" instead of "baba," you still want to sign the words correctly. Keep modeling the correct way to sign if your baby does begin using approximations, and in no time he will be making the signs correctly.

Give an Action Meaning

When a baby first starts saying "dada," he isn't really saying "daddy"; he's simply practicing making sounds. It is our job as parents and teachers to help the child realize that the sound "dada" means "daddy." After a few times of repeating back "daddy" when he says "dada"—and perhaps pointing at a picture or Daddy himself—he will begin to link the sound "dada" to his dad. We can do the same thing for signing. If your baby is clapping, ask him if he wants "more" of something. By responding to that action in a meaningful way, by giving him "more," he will begin to link the action to its meaning.

Building on the Basics

When you teach your baby signs, focus on introducing single signs with single words. Don't try to sign two words together. Start with the basics and then build from there. Once your little one has learned the basic word vocabulary, then you can begin to put those words together. Think of signing as building blocks. You need to start with the first skill, the single sign, before adding to it.

When your baby first begins playing with blocks, you introduce him to one and then show him how to stack them. You know he isn't going to have the skills to place one block on top of the other yet, but you also know that, in time, as he develops, he will. Your child will keep practicing, and one day you'll see him put one block on top of another, then another, and so on. Similarly, when you are teaching ASL, you start with a simple word that is related to an object that your baby is extremely familiar with, such as "milk," "food," "mommy," and "daddy." Once your baby starts to sign that word, take the opportunity to build on it. If your baby learns to sign "milk," you can introduce new connecting signs to your baby. This would include words such as "warm," "bottle," "more," "finish," "fridge," "like," and "good." When you teach your baby combinations of the same word, you are not only increasing his vocabulary, but you are also teaching his new ways to use that sign. Eventually, your child will start coming up with word or sign combinations of his own.

You can continue to build on your child's signing vocabulary as he grows. Some babies develop well over twenty signs before they are able to say one word. Building on the signing vocabulary will help expand your child's language skills even after she begins speaking. Many children have trouble pronouncing words correctly, and signing will definitely help bridge this challenging gap. You will also find that your child will enjoy learning new words in sign language, as it is a fun and engaging way to interact with each other.

Beyond Basic Signs

Signing basic words as a communication tool is a great start for your baby. But do you know you can do so much more with signing to help your child as he grows? Signing can be very useful to children when they are learning their ABCs or when they are learning to read. It can be a great tool to use long after they begin talking.

The ASL Alphabet

The main benefit of learning the ASL alphabet is that it will make it much easier for you to learn and remember specific signs. In our classes, the first thing we do is teach parents the alphabet. Even if they aren't going to teach it to their babies, the parents find it useful to know the letters in order to make it easier to remember words. For example, the sign for water uses your *W hand* shape tapping on your mouth. Most of the colors use the first letter of the word: blue uses the letter *b*, yellow uses *y*, green uses *g*, and so forth.

Babies love songs that have actions put to them. Think about "Itsy Bitsy Spider" and "Twinkle, Twinkle, Little Star." Children prefer them because of the actions that you do when you sing the songs. When you sing and sign your ABCs to your baby, you are adding another fun element to the experience. I used to sing and sign the ABCs to my daughter, and when she started signing them, she would hold her hand up and wiggle her fingers like she was trying to imitate me.

Signing the letters of the alphabet can also be a fun game to play when you are waiting with your children and you have nothing with which to entertain them. I used to play a game of "guess the letter" with my daughter. We would also play "I spy" and give hints using the letters. We'd sign the color of the thing we were spying, and then slowly give hints until the person found it. We'd normally end up signing the first letter it started with and then we could get it.

Both of my children were also more interested in learning the ASL alphabet letters than the written ones. They could both identify the ASL alphabet before they could identify written letters. This made teaching them the written ones much easier. When my daughter would occasionally be stuck on a letter, I would sign it to her and she would remember it more than if I had said it to her. Because both written and sign letters are visual, it was easier for her to recall the written letters from her brain using ASL cues.

Signing Boosts Reading Skills

Dr. Marilyn Daniels, former professor at Penn State University, has done extensive research on the effects of sign language with typically developing children. Her findings have been published in academic journals and also in her book *Dancing with Words: Signing for Hearing Children's Literacy*.

She has published five studies that indicate that incorporating ASL in early childhood education improves the receptive English vocabulary of typical young hearing learners to a statistically significant degree. Dr. Daniels received great results from her observation of fourteen hearing preschoolers. Her research indicated that sign language positively influences children who need to learn and retain English.

To learn more, she set up a research study using students from an early childhood program in Maryland. She wanted to discover whether adding sign language to the curriculum in prekindergarten classes would improve the students' comprehension of English vocabulary.

Four classes of similar size and economic background were tested. Two classes included sign language in their curriculum, and the other two classes used a traditional method of teaching with no sign language.

The teachers had similar qualifications and evaluations, and prior to the ASL intervention, there was basically no difference in the grades their students earned on kindergarten placement tests.

The Peabody Picture Vocabulary Test (PPVT-R) was used to test the students to determine the effect of signing on English acquisition. This test is given orally, so no reading is required. Participants are shown pictures and they respond to the questions based on the four choices of pictures. An examiner might ask the student, "Which person is riding a bike?" and the student would respond by giving the number to the corresponding picture. In this particular study, the students who used sign language scored fifteen points higher than those with no sign instruction.

Children who use sign language also become excited about learning their letters and words. Dr. Daniels writes that "heightening a child's interest in learning to read may be the strongest contribution sign language will make to the reading process."

You may come across many alphabet books with a letter along with a picture representing the letter. For instance, an apple represents the letter *a*. You will often find large alphabet charts similar to this in preschool or grade-school classrooms.

Sign language can work in much the same way as these alphabet charts. Not only can you show the letter *a* and a picture of an apple, but you can show the sign for apple and the manual alphabet letter for *a*.

Dr. Daniels writes of the advantages of using the manual alphabet in order to teach letters. In school, children are normally taught the alphabet by little key cards that are taped above the blackboard. In my class it was an alphabet train, and in my daughter's class it is a rocket ship with the alphabet stringing along behind it. When you teach the alphabet, you teach the sound of each letter, and then that sound the children learn can help prompt reading words. For example, if a student knows the sound the letter *c* makes, then that might help to trigger her sounding out the word "cat." By teaching the ASL hand shape alphabet, you are giving children the same memory cue, but they are actually able to take that memory cue with them. The key cards of the alphabet are helpful at school, where students can look up and see them, but what happens when children are in another environment? By teaching the manual alphabet using the same principle as the key card letters, you are enabling children to always have those memory cues with them.

Dr. Daniels has also found that students who know the manual alphabet are easily able to transfer that knowledge into printed letters. It brings an awareness of the letters and students are able to use the same memory cues for sounding out letters as they are when writing them.

According to Dr. Daniels, finger spelling and signing can also enhance your child's memory since it involves both physical and thinking activity. Signs function as built-in pictures to accompany a text. This reinforces the learning for your child by providing clear symbols for words and letters.

Benefits for Schoolchildren

. . . .

I just wanted to send you a note and thank you for what you've posted on YouTube and your Web site. I am signing with my daughter and we are beginning to see the fruits of our labor. At eight months, she is now signing "milk" when she actually wants milk. She is very intent when she watches my hands and will often look at her hands as if to say, "How do I do that?" I've done a lot of research on signing with young children and I knew it was something I wanted to do with my daughter. At first, some (notably my mother-in-law) were skeptical. Now that she's seen Emily sign for milk, I think (and hope) she realizes how much signing will help Emily throughout her life. I also have used your ABC phonics song in my classroom. My first-graders did not know their letters or sounds. When I stumbled across your video on YouTube, I showed it to my class the next day. The students will actually sing the song out on the playground, and one of my students who was having trouble sounding out words is now able to blend phonemic words if I show him the signs. It's made him feel successful because I can sign (in a sneaky way so the other kids don't notice) and he can blend simple words like "get," "cat," and "dog." Now we are working on getting him to connect the sign to the printed letter. I don't know what I would have done with this little guy without your video. He is performing at a preschool level three-quarters of the way through first grade. My class really jumped on board with signing and they now know sixty-five signs (including the alphabet). They will sign to each other, to me, and are teaching their friends in other classes. I love that I can give them directions to get their pencils and go sit at their desks without saying a word. Again, thanks so much for what you do. The area I live in doesn't have much in the way of sign language resources, so your videos, combined with several Web sites and books, have been a great help.

Thanks.

—Tracey M.

How I Taught My Daughter to Read at Two and a Half

When I started teaching my daughter the ASL alphabet, I began by simply singing and signing the ABCs. She loved watching my hand move as I sang the alphabet song and she would often try to sign along by moving her hands randomly. Once she could sing her ABCs by herself from start to finish, I slowly introduced her to the ASL letters over several months.

I started by showing her the letter *a* with my hand and saying to her, "This is the letter *a*." Then I would hold it up and ask her what letter it was, and she would say, "*a*" Then I added the letter *b*. I would do the same thing and ask her what letter it was. I would go back and forth between *a* and *b*. I didn't move on until she knew what both letters were without mixing them up or guessing. Then I added the letter *c* and would do the same thing, going back and forth from *a* to *b* to *c,* asking her what each letter was. I never moved on to the next one until I knew she had the new one down pat. Once we went through the whole alphabet in order, I would then begin to quiz her out of order. I would hold up random letters and she would tell me what they were.

Once she was able to understand what each letter was out of order, I knew I could put the sounds (phonics) of the letters to them. I would teach her the sounds of the letters using the same process as I did when teaching her the letters, working very slowly and not overwhelming her with too many letters at once. When I saw that she knew all of her letters out of order, I began putting three-letter words together.

To teach her how to read, I would hold up letters and ask her to make the sound for them as I was forming a word. For example, for the word "cat," I would hold up the letter *c* and she would make the sound for *c,* then I would hold up the letter *a* and she would make that sound, and finally I'd hold up *t* and she'd make that sound. Then I would hold them all up again but move them a little faster as she was sounding out each word. I'd do this a couple of times, going faster each time, until she realized she was saying (reading) the word "cat." She would get so excited when she read a word. She had no interest in doing this with written words; she only wanted to play the game with our hands.

This was another fun game we could play when we were out. We would often play the reading/spelling game on long trips or while we were waiting for food at a restaurant. This is an activity that engages your child in a fun and interactive manner. You don't need any special equipment, just your hands and your brains.

My daughter's ability to spell words before she could write them made the transition to written letters and words very easy for her. I remember one day when she was writing out her letters, she stopped for a second, looked at her hand, made the letter *e* with her hand, and then wrote it down. It was clear that her knowing the hand-shape letters helped her when she was printing. She didn't have to look at any other example text, as she always had her hands on her and could reference them if need be. Clearly, there was a link to the look of a written letter and the hand-shape letter in her mind. To her, they were the same thing; one was equal to the other, not two different letters. It's just like students can read an uppercase *a* and a lowercase *a* and know that they are the same letter. Fireese could look at her *A hand* shape and know that it is the same as a written letter *a*. The wonderful thing about teaching the manual alphabet to children is that they will always have it with them. They won't ever have to look for a sheet of paper to use as a reference.

Routines and Behavior Management

Sign language can be a great tool for setting up routines or managing behaviors in a subtle way. When I was a teacher, I used sign language to set up routines and establish the expectations I had of the students. When we moved from one subject or task to another, I would stand up and give sign instructions to my class. From the first day of school this was a routine I had in place. They knew when I stood up to stop what they were doing and look at me; if they didn't, then they would miss my instructions. I found this much more orderly than my class was prior to using sign language. Before incorporating signs into my classroom routine, I would verbally ask students to move on to another task. Many of them would keep their heads down and continue working or would rustle around doing something else. Many times it would result in my calling a student out or raising my voice to get them to respond the way I had initially asked. With sign language, the class was very quiet and each child had to have his eyes on me. I never had to raise my voice or call a student out and embarrass him in front of his peers.

Another time sign language came in handy was during assemblies. Our principal had a very strict policy that students were not to get up and leave an assembly. It never failed that during an assembly students would get up and ask to use the restroom or get a drink. I would see a child get up from the middle of the room, walk in front of others, and possibly horse around en route to asking the teacher if he could go get a drink. The teacher would tell him no and make him sit back down. This, of course, caused undue disruption during a time when the students were supposed to be sitting quietly. My class knew that they were not to get up unless they asked me, and they could do so easily through the use of signs. I always had one student ask for a drink or to go to the toilet. They could easily sign "toilet" or "water" to me. My answer was always no, but they could always tell me if it was a restroom emergency or not. I could then make the call to let the student go or not. If I did, then he could simply get up and leave to use the restroom. There was no need for him to come over and whisper loudly to me, disrupting the students around us. Instead, we could have a quiet interaction by using signs. And of course my students loved learning the key signs, as they felt like they were in a secret club with passwords that only our class knew.

Signing is also great to help with managing the home or loud situations with your children when you are out and about. Once I was at a water park with my daughter and it was very noisy. She was lined up to go on a slide and was asking me if she was big enough to go down it. I was near the pool with the baby and was having difficulty hearing her. She was yelling and getting more frustrated because I didn't understand her and she didn't want to lose her place in line. She then had a big smile on her face and began to sign the question to me. She simply signed the words "me+go+yes+no." This simple sentence got her question across and I was easily able to respond to her. When she got down to the bottom of the slide, she said to me, "See, Mom. Isn't signing cool! And it's not just for babies."

I would also be able to use it as a gentle reminder to my children to use their manners if we were at friends' or family members' houses. Sometimes they would forget to say "please" and "thank you," and I could easily, and discreetly, sign the word to them, and then they would say it. I loved this because I wasn't embarrassing them by calling them out in front of the person; I could subtly remind them without anyone knowing.

Potty Training Across a Park

. . . .

What I love about sign language is that you can use it to communicate with your children in a situation where you might want some privacy. This came into play when we were potty training my son. If we were out at the park, I could easily get his attention and make the sign "toilet." I like this method much better than having to yell across the playground to him in a loud voice saying, "Do you have to go potty?" I found that using the sign "toilet" was much less embarrassing for both of us in a situation like this. Interestingly enough, I learned that when I did try and use words to ask him if he had to use the restroom while we were at the playground, I was often met with blank stares. It seemed that by using the sign, he was able to process the question I was asking him more easily.

—BARB A.

. . . .

Bumps in the Road

Getting over Difficulties

Recognition Before Signing

You have to remember that seeing how to sign is different than being able to sign. Your child needs to be exposed to signs for a little while before she will be able to make them. She may understand what your sign means but may not realize that she too can make the sign—and get a response from you. This is something you'll have to teach your child. You can do this by gently taking your baby's hand and showing her how to make the sign. She will soon realize that she can make the same action you are making and you will respond to her.

Baby Is Not Making Eye Contact

You may be concerned if you are having a hard time getting your baby to look at you when you sign, or to pay attention to the sign you are trying to teach. Don't worry. You'd be surprised at how much babies are able to pick up in their peripheral vision. They will learn even if they aren't focused directly on your hands. To help get your baby to focus on you when signing, try sitting face-to-face. Some kids love sitting in a high chair, and this can be a good way to get that direct contact. This is a great time to teach signs: you are facing her and she is watching you and is interested in what you are doing. If you are using a high chair, it's also a great time to teach food signs. You can also try signing a book to her while she enjoys a snack.

Staying Motivated

If you are feeling unsure about the signing process, you may want to join a signing class or a group with other parents who are signing. Exposing your baby to a group of children whose parents also sign with them is a nice way for your baby to pick up signing. If she is exposed to this type of playgroup with some frequency, she'll see that signing isn't just something done in your house. This is also a great way for you to stay motivated. You will have a chance to see other babies' progress and learn new signs. If you are with a group of other parents who sign with their babies, then you are more likely to feel inspired to keep signing with your child. You may also want to join our My Smart Hands baby-sign-language Facebook group to get tips and tricks that other parents have used when teaching their babies sign language.

You need to stay motivated with signing, even if your child doesn't seem to be picking it up as fast as you would like. You can put up signs around your house to remind you. Put the "change diaper" sign near the change table, a "bath" sign in the bathroom, and so forth. This will help encourage you when you feel like you are living a one-sided signing story.

If your baby doesn't seem to be learning the signs you are teaching, and you've been consistently using those signs for several months, then try adding in a new sign. I had a mom in my class who only signed "milk" with her child, and she had been doing so for many months with no sign back from him. I suggested that she try another sign. She came into class the next week, amazed that he started signing "eat," "dog," "more," and "fish" in just seven days. He was just not interested in signing "milk" for some reason. I spoke to her more than a year later and she said he never did sign "milk." Don't mix up too many words, but you can switch to something that your child might be more interested in.

Don't Get Frustrated, Make It Fun!

Don't consider signing as a lesson that has to be taught. Rather, make it something that is naturally incorporated into your day. This natural exposure will be a better learning style for your baby than sitting down and trying to teach a sign.

If your child seems to be frustrated or uninterested in signing, then simply stop signing at that moment and do something else. You can easily sign again with your child when the time is appropriate. Maybe play on the floor with her and take advantage of teaching her a new sign for something she is interested in. You don't want signing to be associated with negative feelings; it should be fun.

Make sure that you show excitement and give praise to your child if she tries to sign. I would often take my son's hands and make a sign and would respond to that sign in an excited voice.

For example, if I was feeding him, I would take his hands and make the sign "more." I would then say, "More? You want more? Sure, you can have more!" while making the sign with his hands and saying "more" in an upbeat and happy voice. Babies love encouragement, and they love the feeling of making you happy. This is great motivation for a baby.

Mixing Up Signs or Stopping Altogether

It sometimes happens that when babies start to sign they confuse signs, or they use one sign for several words. When my daughter first started eating solid food, she would confuse the sign "milk" to mean "eat," "drink," "thirsty," "more," "want," and any other word associated with being hungry or thirsty. This is a very common thing for babies to do when they are first learning how to sign. Because she only had the sign "milk," she used it for anything that was food related. It was at this time when I knew it was time to start introducing new signs to her. Now she needed to know the signs for more, eat, hungry, etc. As her thought process and word comprehension grew, I knew it was the right time to also expand on her signing vocabulary.

There may also be a time when your child will stop signing altogether. I've had many parents e-mail me, concerned that their baby has stopped signing after she had mastered signing several words. This is a very common phenomenon with babies who have just reached a developmental milestone, or are sick or teething. Developmental milestones sometimes affect other aspects of the baby's life. For example, when a child first learns to crawl, her nap schedule may be disrupted because when you put her in the crib at nap time, all she's interested in doing is crawling around. Similarly, when the child first learns how to pull herself up from a seated position, she won't know how to get back down. When you put her in her crib for a nap and she pulls herself up, she becomes stuck and you have to go in and help her down. She may pull herself up several times before she finally falls asleep. Once she masters this milestone, she will then fall back into an easy sleep routine. The same goes with signing. You'll find that if your baby does stop, she'll soon pick it up again once she's past that particular milestone. Make sure not to give up on the signing at this time. If you continue to sign with her, then she'll quickly get back into the signing routine with you.

Be Patient and Don't Give Up!

Some babies may respond to sign language right away, while others may take a while.

Parents sometimes give up on signing too early, just when their child is about to make their first sign. I have never seen a child not sign whose parents were consistent and didn't give up. Getting to the first sign takes the longest time and is the most difficult experience; after that, it all becomes much easier. Many babies will sign their second word faster than they did their first. It's like a light bulb comes on and they realize that their actions have meaning.

Because signing doesn't necessarily feel natural, like speaking does, it can feel like you are doing it for a long time without any results. Keep in mind how long it can take for a baby to speak his first word. Even if your baby says a word before a sign, you will still find the benefits of using sign language quite useful. Children don't always pronounce words clearly; signing allows for a greater understanding of words. If you give up on signing because you feel words are just around the corner, you'd be missing out on all of the advantages signing has with toddlers and even older children.

What If Others Don't Sign with My Baby?

It's best if you can get everyone to sign with your baby, but this might not be practical. Your spouse may be reluctant to sign, your parents may be skeptical, and your day care provider may not know how to do it. There are many reasons why people may not want to sign to your baby. If in the early months you are the primary caregiver, then you will definitely be the person who will be exposing your child to signing consistently. If you have someone looking after your child and they don't sign with her, or they don't do it with any consistency, that's still okay. You will still be able to sign successfully with your baby. As long as you remain consistent, your baby will continue to link your actions to the words you are introducing and will associate signing with you. I can tell you that once your baby starts signing, all the people who care for her will want to get on board quickly.

Getting on Board
. . . .

When I first started signing with our daughter, my husband was very supportive of the idea. However, he rarely signed with her. I'm not sure if he kept forgetting or he was just lazy. It wasn't until my daughter started signing back that he really picked up the signing. One night I went out and left him at home with our daughter. It was dinnertime, and she was signing to him and he didn't know what she was signing. She kept doing the same sign over and over and kept getting more and more frustrated with

*him. I got a frantic call from my husband trying to describe the
sign from the other end of the phone. I couldn't help but chuckle
to myself. Here was our little baby clearly communicating with
her dad, and he was the one getting frustrated. She was signing
"apple" to him. He hadn't seen her sign that word yet, so he
wasn't sure what she wanted. Finally, he was able to respond to
her, and she was happy he finally "got it." From that point on,
my husband made a concerted effort to learn all her signs and to
sign with her. He became very consistent.*

—LAURA BERG

. . . .

I find that when caregivers are looking after a child who is signing, it makes their life much easier if they learn the signs and use
them with the child. They quickly realize that signing with her and
being able to respond to her wants make their job much easier. So
even though in the beginning people may not be consistently introducing signs to your child, they will soon change their minds
when they see the benefits it can bring.

Don't let people's lack of support for your efforts to sign with
your baby deter you from signing with her. You can be successful
regardless of the support you get from those around you.

How Can I Help My Family and Caregivers Sign with My Baby?

The first thing to do is to talk to your family members or caregivers about the benefits of signing. Your child's caregiver might not be
aware of the benefits of signing with a baby and may not fully

understand why you are choosing to introduce her to sign language. By explaining the benefits, you may help them to see why you are using sign language. Maybe start by asking them to introduce just one sign to your baby on a regular basis. For example, if you are asking your mom to use a sign with your baby, you may encourage her to use the sign "grandma" or "I love you." This will make it easier for family members to learn how to sign with your baby. You can also remind caregivers of the signs that you'd like them to use. Don't assume that they're going to remember all of the signs. Once your family members and caregivers get a response from your child, they'll want to pick up more signs to use with her.

If day care providers are taking care of your child, ask them to use key signs with him. This is to their advantage. If your baby is signing, it will make it a lot easier for the providers to understand what your baby wants. Initially, the day care teacher might be hesitant to use signs because she is unfamiliar with them. Just as you did with your family members, you may want to explain the benefits of using sign language with babies. Nowadays more and more people in day cares and preschools are aware of the benefits of using sign language with children and are incorporating sign language into their programs. If your child's day care or preschool hasn't yet begun to sign with the children, this is a great opportunity for you to introduce them to signing.

An easy thing that you can do in order to make it simple for the day care provider to sign with your baby is to print off examples of the signs that your child uses regularly. In the beginning, you may want to introduce a couple of the key signs to your caregiver. Pick the important ones that you think would be useful to your child, such as "milk," "more," "eat," and "finished." Once your caregiver becomes comfortable using those signs, you can add more.

Tips for Caregivers

1. Explain to them why you are signing with your baby. Discuss the benefits of doing so. Signing will make their life easier!

2. Ask your caregiver to start with just one sign. She might be intimidated to sign with your baby, so asking her to use just one sign will help her to get comfortable with signing.

3. Remind your caregiver of the sign. Don't assume that she will remember to do it. She may not want to ask you how to sign a word. At the beginning, talk to her about the sign. Ask how it went and remind her of how to do the sign.

4. Post signs around your house or give a sheet to your child-care provider. If the sign "change diaper" is above your change table, then it will be simpler for your caregiver to remember to make the sign before she changes a diaper.

5. Remember, this is your child and your caregiver should respect your wishes. It is completely reasonable for you to ask the provider to participate in a parenting style that you have chosen for your baby. If you opted to raise your child as a vegetarian, then it is acceptable for you to ask your caregiver not to not give your child meat. You should feel completely comfortable asking your caregiver to sign simple words with your child. You are doing this to make life easier for your baby.

Activities

Sign Language and Music

Music has been shown to have a powerful effect on memory. Do you remember being in school and studying for a test and trying to think up rhymes or little songs to help you remember the thing you were trying to memorize? The easiest way for children to remember the word "Mississippi" is by singing a song or chant M –I-SS –I-SS- I-PP-I. By putting signs to songs, you are tapping into two learning styles and therefore giving the brain a great workout. Music helps us remember information and recall specific memories, feelings, and emotions.

So why not incorporate American Sign Language with singing? Children love to dance and sing, so signing during these activities is a perfect way to teach while having fun.

You've probably sung such songs as "Itsy Bitsy Spider" and "Twinkle, Twinkle, Little Star" with your child. Some of these songs already have actions, but you can easily replace those actions with signs that match the words of the songs. Other songs have no standard actions, but you can go ahead and start using sign language along with the music regardless. As well as helping your child learn the signs, signing while singing also helps to learn the song. The child can anticipate the words that are coming by seeing the words as you sign them.

Importance of Fun Activities When Teaching ASL

We now know the importance of making learning fun. Children tend to engage and retain more when an activity is fun. Long past are the days of having students sit at a desk and take notes all day long. Fun, high-participation activities take place in schools and home-learning environments.

Studies have shown that pressuring children to learn can have a negative impact on the learning goal. The child's mind should be encouraged to develop a healthy attitude toward learning; it's the same for learning ASL. If a child thinks of ASL as another obligation he has to perform, his interest in it will be diminished.

Children sometimes find it hard to concentrate, so it can help to capture their interest by relating ASL to activities that they love. If you use sign language with activities that you wouldn't normally use, then the activity becomes more engaging to the child. Children in general tend to be very active. By adding movement and ASL to a game, for instance, you allow your child to be active in the game, even a simple game of cards. You can easily add signs along with the game to engage the child more. This is especially good for children who have difficulty sitting and concentrating on one task. Because you have them moving their hands and using their brains through signing, you are giving them an activity that involves their bodies, while at the same time they are able to still sit and concentrate on the task at hand. In this chapter you will discover many games that can accommodate a signing component. These games are more fun when signing is added.

Colors can also help when teaching younger children. Research shows that the brain loves colors, which can invoke many powerful feelings and impressions. When teaching your child colors, you can link those colors to the ASL signs, giving your child another cue for remembering the color. When I first started teaching my children their colors, I taught them the words along with the signs. When they forgot a color, they would look at me and I would sign it. The signing cue I would use to help them recall the word was extremely useful for them to learn their colors. They both learned the signs for the colors before the words.

By incorporating sign language into game play you create a more active, participatory environment.

Sign Language with Songs

Singing and signing go together naturally. Most children's songs have motions that go with them; keep in mind, however, that these are not always actual signs. While signing and singing, choose one or two words to sign for each song instead of signing all the words. Use words that occur frequently in the song to help with word recognition through repetition. Here are a few examples. The words in capitals are the suggested words to sign.

Itsy Bitsy Spider
The itsy bitsy SPIDER
Climbed up the WATER spout.
Down came the RAIN
And washed the SPIDER out.

Out came the SUN
And dried up all the RAIN.
And the itsy bitsy SPIDER
Climbed up the spout AGAIN.

Old MacDonald
OLD MacDonald had a FARM
E, I, E, I, O
And on his FARM he had a _____
E, I, E, I, O
With a _____ (make the sound of the animal while signing)
    here and a
____ _____ there, here a _____ there a _____
    everywhere a _____.
OLD MacDonald had a FARM
E, I, E, I, O.
    Animal suggestions:
    Cat, cow, duck, horse, dog, sheep, pig, etc.

Row, Row, Row Your Boat
Row, row, row your BOAT
Gently down the STREAM
Merrily, merrily, merrily, merrily [sign "HAPPY"]
Life is but a DREAM.

Twinkle, Twinkle, Little Star
Twinkle, twinkle little STAR
How I WONDER what you are
Up above the WORLD so high
Like a DIAMOND in the sky

Twinkle, twinkle little STAR
How I WONDER what you are.

Baa, Baa, Black Sheep
Baa, baa, black SHEEP,
Have you any wool?
YES sir, YES sir,
Three bags FULL.
One for my MASTER,
One for my dame (LADY),
And one for the little BOY
Who lives down the LANE.
Baa, baa, black SHEEP
Have you any wool?
YES sir, YES sir,
Three bags FULL.

Mary Had a Little Lamb
Mary had a little LAMB,
Little LAMB, little LAMB,
Mary had a little LAMB,
Its fleece was WHITE as SNOW.
Everywhere that Mary (GIRL) went,
Mary (GIRL) went, Mary (GIRL) went,
Everywhere that Mary (GIRL) went
The LAMB was sure to go.
It followed her to SCHOOL one day,
SCHOOL one day, SCHOOL one day.
It followed her to SCHOOL one day,
which was against the rules.

It made the children LAUGH and PLAY,
LAUGH and PLAY, LAUGH and PLAY,
It made the children LAUGH and PLAY,
To see a lamb at SCHOOL.

Five Green Speckled Frogs
FIVE little speckled FROGS
SAT on a speckled log
EATING some most delicious grubs (BUG).
ONE jumped into the pool
Where it was nice and cool (COLD)
Then there were FOUR green
  speckled FROGS.
FOUR little speckled FROGS
SAT on a speckled log
EATING some most delicious grubs (BUG).
ONE jumped into the pool
Where it was nice and cool (COLD)
Then there were THREE green
  speckled FROGS.
THREE little speckled FROGS
SAT on a speckled log
EATING some most delicious grubs (BUG).
ONE jumped into the pool
Where it was nice and cool (COLD)
Then there were TWO green speckled FROGS.
TWO little speckled FROGS
SAT on a speckled log
EATING some most delicious grubs (BUG).
ONE jumped into the pool

Where it was nice and cool (COLD)
Then there was ONE green speckled FROG.
ONE little speckled FROG
SAT on a speckled log
EATING some most delicious grubs (BUG).
ONE jumped into the pool
Where it was nice and cool (COLD)
Then there were NO green speckled FROGS.

Days of the Week

Tune: "My Darling Clementine"
SUNDAY, MONDAY, TUESDAY, WEDNESDAY,
    THURSDAY, FRIDAY, SATURDAY,
SUNDAY, MONDAY, TUESDAY, WEDNESDAY,
    THURSDAY, FRIDAY, SATURDAY.

Days of the Week

Tune: "Addams Family" theme song
Days of the WEEK (clap, clap)
Days of the WEEK (clap, clap)
Days of the WEEK, days of the WEEK,
Days of the WEEK (clap, clap).
There's SUNDAY and there's MONDAY
There's TUESDAY and there's WEDNESDAY
There's THURSDAY and there's FRIDAY and then there's
    SATURDAY.
Days of the WEEK (clap, clap)
Days of the WEEK (clap, clap)
Days of the WEEK, days of the WEEK,
Days of the WEEK (clap, clap).

On Top of Spaghetti

On top of SPAGHETTI, all covered with CHEESE,
I lost my poor MEATBALL, when somebody SNEEZED.
It rolled off the TABLE and onto the FLOOR,
And then my poor MEATBALL rolled out of the DOOR.
It rolled in the GARDEN and under a BUSH,
And then my poor MEATBALL was nothing but MUSH.
The MUSH was as tasty, as tasty could be,
And then the next SUMMER, it grew into a TREE.
The TREE was all covered, all covered with moss,
And on it grew MEATBALLS, and tomato sauce.
So if you eat SPAGHETTI, all covered with CHEESE,
Hold on to your MEATBALL, whenever you SNEEZE.

One, Two, Three, Four, Five

ONE, TWO, THREE, FOUR, FIVE.
Once I caught a FISH alive.
SIX, SEVEN, EIGHT, NINE, TEN.
Then I let it go AGAIN.
WHY did you let it go?
Because it BIT my finger so.
Which finger did it BITE?
This little finger on my right.

Blue

Tune: "Are You Sleeping?"
B-L-U-E
B-L-U-E
That spells BLUE,

That spells BLUE,
The COLOR of the SKY,
The COLOR of the SEA,
BLUE, BLUE, BLUE,
BLUE, BLUE, BLUE.

Green

Tune: "Are You Sleeping?"
G-R-EE-N
G-R-EE-N
That spells GREEN,
That spells GREEN,
The COLOR of the TREES,
The COLOR of the LEAVES,
GREEN, GREEN, GREEN,
GREEN, GREEN, GREEN.

Red

Tune: "The Farmer in the Dell"
R-E-D spells RED,
R-E-D spells RED,
APPLES and TOMATOES too
R-E-D spells RED.

Yellow

Tune: "Twinkle, Twinkle, Little Star"
YELLOW is the COLOR of the SUN
SHINING DOWN on everyone.
Y-E-L-L-O-W

Y-E-L-L-O-W
YELLOW is the COLOR of the SUN
SHINING DOWN on everyone.

Teaching with Equipment

Teaching ASL with Toys

Children learn better when they're having fun. Therefore, I'd encourage you to make the most of your children's playtime. Playtime is beneficial on many levels. You'll be spending quality time with your child. The parent-child bond will become stronger because you are sharing and participating in your child's special interests. Playtime is a way that your child's creative ability can be put to use. You can allow your baby to explore many different toy or game options and see where his interests are. When children begin imaginary play, it's wonderful to see the boundless creativity your baby has. Playtime is a way for children to experience new things and for you to teach new words for items he's interested in. Signing words that relate to your child's favorite toy (a car, a doll, a ball) or book is an effortless way to increase your baby's sign vocabulary.

Teaching ASL with Books

Books are also a great way to teach your child signs. When you read and sign a book, you are allowing your child to participate more fully in the reading experience. For example, if you read a book you may ask your child to point to certain things, but that's the extent of his participation. When you read and sign, he becomes much more involved. When you read and sign a book, you end up saying the words more often than if you simply read it. When reading you may say something like, "Can you point to the bear? Yes, that's the bear!" saying the word "bear" twice. When you read and sign you might say something like, "Can you point to the bear? Yes, that's the bear! Can you show me the sign for bear? This is the sign for bear [while you sign the word]. Let me help you make the sign 'bear' [taking his hands and signing 'bear']. Yes! That's the sign for bear!" In this case you have used the word "bear" six times. Without necessarily realizing it, you are exposing your child to repetitive language, allowing him to pick up on words faster.

As your child grows older, you can play games while reading. You can sign a word and ask her to find what you are signing. Or you can say the word and ask your child to show you the sign.

I really enjoyed reading and signing at the same time with my children. It made the reading experience last longer, making me slow down and really focus on the things in the book instead of simply flying through it. And I loved that reading and signing allowed them to participate more in the story, making it more engaging for them.

Teaching ASL Through Flash Cards

Flash cards make teaching sign language similar to teaching through reading. I really enjoy using flash cards with both of my children. I liked the fact that the cards focused on one word and one picture. There were no stories to follow; we could simply focus on the vocabulary the cards had to offer.

I don't recommend using flash cards in the traditional sense, where you sit the child down and quiz her by holding up each card, but if your child enjoys this type of play, then go ahead and use the flash cards this way. I like to use them in a more casual way. I give a deck of cards to my son and he lays them down in his lap. He pulls out one card at a time and asks me what it is. I show him the sign and say the word at the same time. Eventually, he will hold up the card and then give it to me and make the sign. My daughter loved to lay the cards out in a long row, making a train with them. She would then go back to the first card and make the sign for it and then move down the word "train," showing me all the signs for the words. By allowing your children just to pick up and play with the cards, you are giving them the freedom to explore and make choices.

My favorite flash card story came from an experience with my son (http://www.youtube.com/watch?v=412EXGd6VbA). I'm sitting with him on my lap in a rocking chair. I'm holding on to a pile of flash cards and he is showing me the signs for each card that I pull. He's confidently saying and signing each one. Then I pull out the flash card with the picture of a bed on it. I ask him the sign and he says no. I started laughing because he knows the sign but he just doesn't want to go to bed. He quickly picked a new card in the hopes that I wouldn't think about putting him to bed. It always amazes me how smart these little guys are.

Walks Around the Neighborhood

Apart from the benefits of some fresh air and a change in environment for your baby, walks are one of the best vocabulary builders there are.

When your child can see so many things, it's inevitable that something will grab his attention. Walks can be a good incentive for your child to initiate a conversation. If your baby likes something he sees—for example, a car or a truck, a dog or a bird—it's likely that he will point at it. This will allow you to engage in meaningful conversation with your child. You can also point out specific things you may see and make the signs for those things: bird, tree, car, dog, and cloud, for example.

Going for a Walk

Whenever I would take my son, Braden, out for a walk, we would always talk about the things that we saw and I would show him the signs for those things. I found this to be a great way to incorporate signing into our day. It felt very easy and natural, and Braden really liked our little adventures. I remember the first time he saw a live horse. Braden was not quite one. We were on a walk and a police horse was sauntering along the street. My son became very excited and started signing "book." I thought that was odd and kept looking around for a book. I could not see one anywhere. Then he signed "horse" and "book" together. I realized he was amazed to see a live horse that was the same as the one in one of our books at home. This was when

I saw how truly amazing signing was. Braden was amazed that the horse in our book was now on the street. I would never have known what he was thinking without sign language.

—RONDA M.

. . . .

Fun Games

Alphabet Games

PRACTICE YOUR ALPHABET

The manual alphabet is a good thing to know for several reasons. First, many signs that you will learn are identified by certain letters in the alphabet. For example, the sign for 'water' is made with the *W hand* shape, and the sign for 'uncle' is made with the *U hand* shape. If you know your alphabet, it will be easier to learn signs.

Second, it is a great thing to teach your toddler. You can also teach your child his letters by using the manual alphabet. It is much easier for him to transfer the manual letters into written letters when he gets older. Babies love when actions are put to songs. Your child will love watching you sing and sign the alphabet. You can also play fun spelling games with him when he is older. You can sign simple words and ask what the words are. For example, you can ask, "What does C-A-T spell?" and you can give your child a hint by making the sign for cat. This is a fun, educational game you can play with your child.

SINGING THE ALPHABET SONG

It is a great idea to sing and sign the alphabet with your little one. She will pick it up faster and be more interested if you sign it because children love watching movement. Also, toddlers tend to be visual learners, so they are going to learn the alphabet faster if you say *a* and also show them the sign for *a*.

Once your baby starts talking, you may want to start teaching her how to identify the different letters in the manual alphabet. Start slowly; you can teach them *a, b,* and *c* and once the child is able to identify those letters you can add more. You'll be surprised at how fast a toddler will be able to understand these letters. Once your child learns all the letters, it will be much easier to begin to write them.

ALPHABET ORDER

You can play this game with alphabet blocks or any alphabet letters you have around the house. If you don't have any, you can print them off. Scatter the letters around and then sign a letter and have your child pick it up and put it in a row. Sign another letter and have your child place it beside the first one. You can do this as many times as you like.

An older child can place letters in a row until a word is spelled out. Once the word is spelled, you can ask him if he knows what he's just spelled. If he is even older and able to spell words, you can play the game by spelling a short word and having him pick out the letters to that word.

Family/People Games

PEEKABOO MOMMY AND DADDY GAME

A fun game to play when teaching the signs for mommy and daddy or any other person sign is the peekaboo game. Start by having Daddy holding the baby and Mommy out of the room. Have Daddy say to the baby, "Where's Mommy?" while signing the word "mommy." Make sure he says it in an excited voice and repeats the question a couple of times. Then have Mommy come into the room and say, "Here's Mommy!" while signing "mommy." Daddy can also take baby's hand and help him make the sign "mommy." Then switch places. If you are home alone, you can play this game just after nap time before picking baby up from his crib. You can stand outside the door and ask, "Where is Mommy?" and then jump into the room and say and sign, "Here's Mommy."

PRACTICE FAMILY SIGNS USING
THE FAMILY PHOTO ALBUM

Think of a couple of family members other than Mommy and Daddy whom your baby sees on a fairly regular basis. It can be Grandma and Grandpa, siblings, aunts and uncles. Looking through family photos, you can show your baby the signs for each family member as you go along. You can also make extra prints of these photos and make a signing photo album for your baby. Staple together some thick, colorful paper and glue on the pictures. You can write each person's title—for example, Grandma—in big bold letters above the photo. Babies love looking at pictures, and this is a fun way to interact with your child and teach the names of each family member. You can also find a book that has family names in it and read and sign it to your child. Start with signing just one word on each page.

Toy Games

Teach Toy Signs

If your child is interested in a particular toy, try to teach him that sign. These are called motivational signs, a sign that your child will be motivated to learn. There's no point in trying to teach your baby a sign that he isn't interested in learning. Instead, look for things that your baby shows interest in and teach that sign. Apart from food, these signs will often be toys. Make sure to use an excited voice and be repetitive. For example, if your baby is playing with a ball, you can say, "This is a ball" and show the sign "ball." Repeat this activity a number of times. You can also pick up the ball and say, "Mommy has the ball" while signing "mommy" and then "ball." Try to pick one or two new toy signs each week (or more if your baby is picking them up fast). Again, the more consistent you are when signing with your baby, the faster he will pick it up.

PICK THE ITEM

When you are playing with your baby, you can pick two items you are teaching the signs for. Maybe it's a car and a ball. You can place the two items on the floor in front of your baby. Then ask your baby, "Where is the car?" while making the sign "car." Encourage him to pick up the toy car and be excited when he does.

Then you can put the car back and sign the other one and see if your child can pick that one up. In the beginning you'll have to help your baby pick the toy, but soon he'll be able to do it on his own. Your baby will like this simple game. The older your baby gets, the more toys you can add.

RACE GAME

Take certain items that your child knows the sign for and put them on the other side of the room. You sign an item and she runs and picks it up and brings it back to you. Then you sign the next one until she's picked them all up. See how fast they can do this game. Children love being timed and doing races. They find it fun to be able to improve their times.

MYSTERY BAG

Put a toy in a bag and have your child stick his hands in and feel what it is. Once he knows what it is, ask him what the sign is. To make the game a little harder, add more than one item and have him sign all the things in the bag. If you put two cars that he knows really well in a bag, and then see if he can figure out which color they are based on the shape of the car, get him to sign the color.

WHAT'S MISSING GAME

Have a few toys lying on the floor. Show your child the sign for each item you've laid out. Ask your child to close his eyes and then take one item away. Tell him to open his eyes and ask him to sign the item you've removed. This is a great way for him to practice his memory recall and signing at the same time. You can do the opposite and add items to the group and ask him to sign what was added.

Opposite Pairs

Start with easy opposite pairs such as up and down, on and off, or wet and dry. Find a toy that your child is interested in. Put the toy on something such as a table or chair; show the sign "on" and say, "The ___ [whatever the toy is] is 'on' the table." Then take the toy off the table and sign and say, "The _____ [toy] is 'off' the table."

Here's another activity you can do with opposites. Get two face-cloths, wet one, and keep the other dry. Let your baby pick up and play with the facecloths. Whenever your baby is holding the wet one, you can say, "That facecloth is wet," while making the sign "wet." When holding the dry one, make the sign "dry."

You can pick your baby up and point your finger up, saying "up." Then make the sign "down" and say, "Down." Do this a couple of times and then ask your baby if he wants "up" while signing "up" and see if he'll make the sign. Babies love this up/down game; they will think it is funny being picked up and put down.

Another activity you can do with opposites is sit on the floor with your baby and say, "Mommy is sitting on the floor," making sure to sign the word "sit" while using a very excited voice. Remember, babies respond to the tone of voice. Then stand and say, "Mommy is standing," while signing the word "stand." See if you can get your child to do an action based on what you are signing.

Pick a toy that is big and another that is small. Ask your baby, "Where is the big toy?" while signing "big" and emphasizing that word. Point to the big toy and say, "This is the 'big' toy," while signing "big."

It is easy to teach opposite pairs because these signs are very concrete. Children have an easy time grasping the concept of opposites because they can see when something is on or off, in or out, wet or dry. By adding these fun "opposite games" to your daily playtime, you will find it not only fun and engaging, but also educational.

Games with Books

Practice People Signs Using Books

When introducing people signs, you can start by reading books that have the different people in them: police, fireman, doctor. Also, when you are out for a walk, you may see a police car or fire truck and you can show your baby the signs for them. You can stop and point to the fire truck and say there is a fireman on that truck, while making the sign for fireman. You may also want to teach your baby the sign for doctor and talk about the doctor being our friend, as this will prepare your baby for doctor's visits.

Introduce Color Signs Through Books or Songs

It's fun to teach colors using sign language. You can read books or sing songs that have colors in them and sign along to the song or the book. When you are reading to your child, make sure to show her the signs that go with each color. Just like reading any other book, this activity engages your little one in the learning process. You may even find that your toddler will learn the signs for the colors before she learns the words. Both of my children learned the signs for all the colors first. By teaching the signs along with the words, it allows you to give your child easy cues when she is trying to remember the word for a certain color.

Additionally, you can sing and sign color songs to your baby. There are a few included in this book in the songs section. By singing and signing the colors, you are encouraging your child to learn his colors through the use of music and signs. This is a fun way for your toddler to learn his colors. It's active and engaging, and children love songs and the movements that accompany them.

Teach Seasons and Weather Signs

A great way to teach signs for seasons or weather is through the use of themed books. Find a book that has the different seasons in it and begin to show your child the signs for them and the weather associated with each season. If you are really motivated, you can make a felt board with the four seasons and have different weather conditions that your baby can pick and put on the board. You can sign each thing your little one picks up to place on the board. This is a great activity for toddlers.

If your child is little, you can help him make a weather book. Cut out pictures from a magazine or even print off any pictures you have showing different weather conditions, then glue the pictures to paper and staple them together. Make sure to put the word for each weather situation above each picture in your book—for example, "snow," "rain," "sun." Then you can read and sign the book you've created. My daughter loved making one of these books for her baby brother.

WHAT AM I SIGNING?
Choose a book, sit your baby on your lap, and flip through it. On each page pick one thing to sign. Make the sign and ask your toddler what you are signing. If your child is young, you can help him

by making the sign, then asking him where it is and then helping him point to the item. For example, if you are signing "moon" on the page, then ask your child, "Where is the moon?" while signing "moon." Then take your child's hand and help him point to the moon. Then say, "Yes, that's the moon!" Reinforce the word by making the sign again. For older babies you can ask them to sign something on the page and have you find it. This is a great way to engage your child in his learning versus sitting and simply reading to him.

Create an Emotions Book (or Find One at the Store)

Depending on how creative you are, you might want to create a fun emotions book for your little one in one of two ways. You can take pictures of yourself or your partner (or other family members) making different faces: angry, happy, sad, serious. Staple some thick colorful pages together and glue the pictures on the pages. Above each page you can write the word for the emotion in big, bold letters. Then, when you are reading through the book, you can make the sign for each emotion.

If you don't have time to take photos, find pictures in magazines that show different emotions and glue those in a book. You can label them in the same way as described above.

On the other hand, there are a lot of great books that have very clear descriptions of the different emotions and the appropriate faces to go along with them. As your child gets older and has grasped the concept of emotions and their signs, you can start to introduce more abstract thinking. Ask them questions like, "If Sally didn't share with Sammy, would Sammy be happy or sad?" Then pause and let your little one answer the question. If he doesn't get it at first, you can say, "Sammy would be 'sad' if Sally didn't share with him." Once he's mastered that, you can move on to a more open-ended question that doesn't give an A/B choice, such as "If Suzie and her Mommy are baking a cake, how do you think Suzie feels?"

When your baby gets a little older, you are going to want to introduce more abstract concepts, such as please, thank you, and sorry. You can sit with your son or daughter and ask for the toy that they are playing with by saying, "May I 'please' play with that toy?" while signing "please." Then gently take the toy and say, "Thank you" while signing "thank you."

Games with Cards

Story Board Fun

Using flash cards, you can create a fun story board with your child by lining up several cards. For example, if you have the cards "mommy," "eat," "cookie," "more," and "please," then you can make a fun story that could read: "Mommy bakes yummy cookies that I love to eat. When I finish one, I always say, 'More, please!'" Sign all the flash cards as you tell your story. Then tell it again and have your child sign the words along with you. Then you can tell it a third time and have him sign the words as you get to them on his own. This is a great way to reinforce words you are trying to teach.

Go Fish Game with Signs

For a child who is older, you can play "go fish." Get a deck of cards that have pictures on them instead of numbers. Deal out the cards in the same way you would do with "go fish." The number of cards you decide to use will depend on the age of your child. You can ask her, "Do you have a _____" and then make the sign for the item you are asking for instead of saying the word. If she isn't sure what you are signing, then you can give her a hint. If it's an animal, you can make the sound; if it's a toy, you can describe the shape or color.

Flash Card Order

When you first begin playing this game, just pick two or three cards (depending on the age of your child). If you have three cards, sign all three signs and ask your toddler to put them in order of how you signed them. If you have cards showing a dog, a cat, and a cow, then sign "dog," "cat," and "cow," and your child would have to put the cards in that order. This is a great way for children to practice memory retention. If your little one has trouble at first, then you can sign one at a time and let him put them in order. When he becomes more comfortable with the game, you can add more cards. Make sure to take turns and allow him to be the signer.

Sign of the Week

When teaching new signs, you can create a "sign of the week." Pick a new sign, and then post it on the fridge or someplace all family members will see on a regular basis. Make sure that everyone uses the new sign a few times throughout the week.

Reminder Cards

Make signing cards and stick them on the items around the house so you remember to sign at those "stations." In the bathroom, you can post the signs for bath, duck (if your baby has a rubber ducky), soap, and bubbles. Post whichever words you find useful. Doing this is a great way to help you remember to sign throughout your day.

Outdoor Games

Teaching Weather

Another great way to teach weather signs is when you are out for a walk. If it's summer, you can point out how hot it is in the summer. You can also point out in sign language the beautiful flowers that grow during the summer or the trees, leaves, and birds. You can do the same during the other seasons. If it is winter, you can show your baby the snow and point out that it is cold and white. Take advantage of your walks and show your baby interesting things along the way that you can sign.

Zoo Visits

Take your baby on a trip to a zoo and teach him all of the fun animal signs. See if there are any animals in his favorite books that he may be familiar with. My daughter loved picking out all of the animals in the picture book *Brown Bear, Brown Bear, What Do You See?* We would also try to figure out if we had a book in the house with a particular animal in it. This is a fun game to help your child's recall. You can say, "This is the sign for tiger" while making the sign and showing him the tiger walking around the cage. Then ask, "Do we have a book with a 'tiger' in it?" If you have one and he doesn't remember which one, then give him clues about the book until he remembers. Not only are you reinforcing the sign for tiger, but you are also having him use his brain to recall an item at home.

Games Without Tools

Sing and Sign a Song

Pick your baby's favorite song and sign the key words in it. When you first begin signing the song, you can pick just one word to sign. Then, when your child is familiar with that one sign, you can add more. For example, for the song "Itsy Bitsy Spider," you may want to start by only signing "spider." A few weeks later, you might want to add "rain," then the next week, add "down." This is also a fun way to introduce new signs weekly to your little one.

"I Spy"

Play "I spy," using signs instead of saying what you've found. If you spy a green object, you'd say to your child, "I spy with my little eye something that is [and then sign the word] 'green.'" As your child guesses, you can give him clues using different signs. Or your child could try to guess the item you've spied using signs.

Animal Noises Signs

Make an animal sound and have your baby sign the animal, then switch. Your child makes a sound and you sign it. This is a fun way to see how many animal sounds your little one knows and how many animal signs he has learned. It's also a great way to teach new animal signs to your baby if he doesn't know one.

Action Signs

Sign actions and have him do them; for example, "run," "jump," "sit," "stand," "walk," "stop," "fast," and "slow." This is a great game to play with older children. You can even add emotions. When I play this with my daughter, I do the sign and she makes a face; then we switch. She does the sign and I make a face (happy, scared, sad, and grumpy). My daughter loves this game because she gets me making goofy faces or running and jumping, which seems to really entertain her.

Back Drawing

Draw a letter of the alphabet on your child's back or palm and have him guess what letter you've drawn. Ask him to sign and say the letter. As he advances, you can spell short words and get him to sign it along with you and then tell you the word you've spelled.

Part III

The Dictionary

In the dictionary I will refer to dominant and nondominant hand shapes. If you are right-handed that would be considered your dominant hand. If you are left-handed that would be your dominant hand. When signing, it doesn't matter which hand you use. If you are left-handed you would use your left hand, and if you are right-handed you would use your right hand. Whichever hand you write with is considered your dominant hand. That is the hand that will be predominantly used when making the signs. Signing should feel comfortable to you.

Alphabet

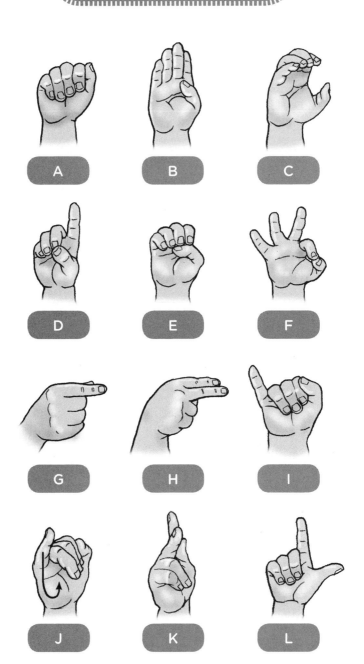

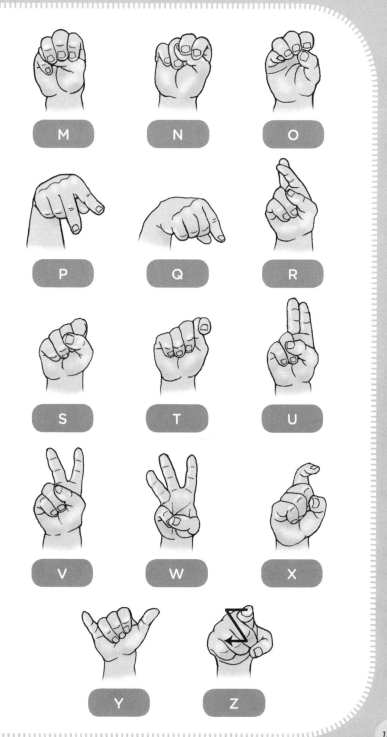

Numbers

1

2

3

4

5

6

7

8

9

10

Colors

Move the tip of your index finger down your lips once, pointing to the color of your red lips.

Red

Open and close your hand in front of your mouth a couple of times like you are squeezing an orange.

Orange

Shake or twist the wrist of your *Y hand* just in front of you.

Yellow

Shake or twist the wrist of your
G hand just in front of you.

Green

Shake or twist your *B hand*.

Blue

Shake or twist the wrist of your
P hand just in front of you.

Purple

Using the middle finger of your *P hand*, swipe it down on your bottom lip. Think of putting pink lipstick on.

Pink

Move your *B hand* down the side of your cheek.

Brown

Wipe your straight index finger along your eyebrow. Think of a big unibrow.

Black

Place the fingertips of your
5 *hand* on your chest and then
pull your hand away from your
chest and fingers together.

White

Seasons

Spring

Use your nondominant *C hand* to represent the ground, and using your dominant *flattened O hand*, move it up through the ground while spreading your fingers open, representing a growing flower.

Summer

Bend your index finger as you move it across your forehead like you are wiping sweat from your brow.

Brush your elbow a couple of times. This represents the leaves falling from trees.

Autumn

Holding your hands in fists and your arms close to your body, shiver like you are cold.

Winter

Days of the Week

Using your *M hand* with palm facing in, move it in a circle in front of you.

Monday

Using your *T hand*, palm facing you, move it in a circle in front of you.

Tuesday

Using your *W hand*, palm facing you, move it in a circle in front of you.

Wednesday

Make the letters *t* and *h* for the TH in Thursday.

Thursday

Using your *F hand*, palm facing you, make a circle in front of you.

Friday

Using your *S hand*, palm facing you, move it in a circle in front of you.

Saturday

Hold your flat hands up with palms facing out, and then drop them down.

Sunday

Hold your nondominant hand flat with the palm facing up, and then tap the fingertips of your bent dominant hand on it. You can repeat this motion a few times.

Again

Hold up your thumb, index finger, and baby finger, and move them slightly back and forth in the air to show an airplane moving.

Airplane

Put both hands up with your palms facing you, and then move your hands in a swift motion so that your palms are facing out. Repeat this motion a couple of times.

(Also see FINISHED on page 194.)

All done

Alligator

Use your bent 5 *hands* and snap them together like an alligator's jaw.

(*Also see* CROCODILE *on page 180.*)

Angry

Hold your 5 *hand* in front of your face and move your fingers in and out, showing your face scrunching up like a grouch.

(*Also see* GRUMPY *on page 205,* MAD *on page 220, or* UPSET *on page 281.*)

Animal

Place the fingertips of your two hands on your chest, and then move your hands in and out as if you are showing lungs breathing.

Put the middle knuckle of your *X hand* shape on your cheek and twist your wrist back and forth. Think of the apple of your cheek.

Apple

Holding your hand flat, palm facing the ground, move your hand in a circle. Think of showing the area out in front of you.

Area

Holding your *A hand* near your jaw, move it in a circular motion. You can also make a twisting motion at the wrist.

Aunt

Brush your elbow a couple of times. This represents the leaves falling from trees.

Autumn

Holding both your hands in the *A hand* shape, slice along your fist where your fingers meet your palm with the thumb of your other *A hand*. Think of cutting an avocado.

Avocado

Put your index finger and thumb together in front of your eye, and then move your fingers apart. Think of your eyes going from closed to open.

Awake

Baby

Cup your arms together as if you are holding a baby, and then rock them back and forth.

Bad

Put your flat hand on your chin, and then move it out and away as if you are throwing something away.

Ball

Put your hands in the shape of a ball and tap them together a few times.

Hold your fists in front of your mouth, and then move them out as you open them. Think of how a balloon would look as you inflate it.

Balloon

Move your hand down your index finger, simulating the peeling of a banana.

Banana

Sign "farm" (page 193) and "house" (page 209) together.

Barn

Bath

Move your fists up and down at the same time on your chest as if you are scrubbing clean.

Batteries

Using your *X hands*, tap your index fingers together. Think of the connections a battery makes.

Bear

Cross your arms and scratch at your shoulders with your "bear" claws.

Beautiful

Using your 5 *hand*, hold it in front of your face, and then swipe your fingers around and down to your chin, closing your hand at the bottom. Think of showing how beautiful your face is.

(Also see PRETTY on page 243.)

Bed

Put your hands together and rest them on the side of your cheek as if you are sleeping on them. You can also use just one hand to make this sign.

Bee

Using the *F hand* shape, put it sharply to the side of your lip, showing a quick "sting," and then swat the "bee" away using the same hand.

Begin

Hold your nondominant hand flat with your palm facing toward you, and then place the index finger of your dominant hand between your index and middle fingers. Make a twisting movement like you are turning a key in a lock. Think of putting a key in the car's ignition and starting it.

(Also see START on page 266.)

Bicycle

Hold your hands as if you are holding on to a bike's pedals and mimic them pedaling. Think of how your legs would pedal a bike.

Big

Start with your hands close together and move them apart. This sign can also be made with bent *L hands* moving apart for large.

(Also see LARGE on page 216.)

Bird

Place your hand in front of your mouth and, using your index finger and thumb, open and close them like a bird's beak opening and closing.

Birthday

Tap the middle finger of your 5 *hand* on your chin and then move it down to your chest. Think that on your birthday you eat birthday cake with the people you love (tapping from close to your mouth to your chest).

Bite

Hold your left hand up and grab on to it quickly with the fingertips of your right hand. Think of your right hand being a mouth biting something.

Wipe your straight index finger along your eyebrow. Think of a big unibrow.

Black

Pretend you are holding on to a blanket and are pulling it up your chest.

Blanket

Shake or twist your *B hand.*

Blue

Boat

Cup your hands in the shape of a boat and bounce forward, showing it floating on the water.

Book

Hold your hands together and open them like a book.

Bottle

Hold your nondominant hand flat, palm facing up, and put your dominant hand on it as if you are holding a bottle and move it upward, outlining the shape of a bottle.

Boy

Open and close your hand up near your forehead, as if you are tapping on the brim of an imaginary baseball cap.

Bread

Pretend one hand is a loaf of bread and use the fingertips of your other hand to "slice" the bread.

Broken

Hold both hands in fists together with the back of your hands facing up. Then "snap" your hands apart so that your fingers are facing each other. Think that you are holding on to a stick and are breaking it in half.

Using two *L hand* shapes, touch your forehead where you make the sign "boy" and then move your hand down to touch your other hand.

Brother

Move your *B hand* down the side of your cheek.

Brown

Hold your fingers together in an *O hand* shape and open and close them as you move them upward. Think of bubbles floating up and popping as they go.

Bubble

Bug

Using your 3 *hand,* put your thumb on your nose and bend and straighten your index and middle fingers. Think of the antennae of a bug.

Bull

Place the back of your *Y hand* on your forehead, indicating the bull's horns.

Bunny

Hold up the index and middle fingers on both your hands, cross your hands in front of your chest, and wiggle your fingers a bit. Think of holding a bunny with its ears flopping.

(Also see RABBIT on page 246.)

This word is normally finger spelled B-U-S. In this version, you take your two *B hands* and place them together with hands facing opposite ways, then move them out showing the length of the bus.

Bus

Cross your hands over each other and link your thumbs together. Wiggle your fingers, mimicking the wings of a butterfly. It looks like a butterfly flying through the air.

Butterfly

Place fingertips of your dominant hand on the palm of your other hand and raise your dominant hand up, showing a cake rising.

Cake

Using your whole hand, pretend to draw the outline of a camel's hump in front of you.

Camel

Place your index finger on your cheek and twist it slightly.

Candy

Move your hands like you are driving a car.

(Also see VAN on page 282.)

Car

Using your *K hands*, place one on top of the other and move them in a circle outward and back in toward you.

Careful

Pretend you are holding a big carrot and are taking a bite.

Carrot

Using your *F hand* shape, pull outward on your cheek as if you are pulling at imaginary whiskers.

Cat

Hold your left arm flat and inch your right hand's index finger along your left arm. Think of a caterpillar crawling along a log.

Caterpillar

Place your index finger near your mouth and bend and extend it a couple of times as you move it across your mouth. Think of chomping on cereal.

Cereal

Using your index and middle fingers on your dominant hand, tap them twice on the index and middle fingers of your nondominant hand. Think of a person taking a seat in a chair.

Chair

Place your dominant fist on top of your nondominant fist, fingers touching. Then move them in a circle, changing their position. The nondominant hand should now be on top.

Change

Place the heels of your palms together and twist back and forth, like you are squishing a cheese slice.

Cheese

Place your hand in front of your mouth and, using your index finger and thumb, open and close them like a bird's beak opening and closing.

(Also see BIRD on page 165.)

Chicken

Tap your hand along a few times as if you are tapping the top of kids' heads.

Children

Move your hand forward as if you are cleaning something off your hand.

Clean

Place the middle finger of your *5 hand* on the side of your head and move it up and out. Think of your brain waves exploding from your head.

(Also see SMART on page 260.)

Clever

Pretending you are holding a cloud above your head, twist your hands as you move them across the sky. Think of a cloud moving through the sky.

Cloud

Tap your fingers on your nose, showing the clown's big red nose.

Clown

Use both hands and pretend you are pulling a coat up over your shoulders.

(Also see JACKET on page 213.)

Coat

Holding your hands in fists and your arms close to your body, shiver like you are cold.

(Also see WINTER on page 288.)

Cold

Flutter or wiggle your fingers at your chin.

Color

Tap your C *hand* in a circular motion up your arm.

Computer

Place the fingertips of your dominant hand on the palm of your flat hand and twist it as if you are cutting out a cookie.

Cookie

Hold your C *hand* at the side of your head and wiggle a couple of times back and forth. Some people make this sign with the C *hand* near the forehead for a male cousin and near the jaw for a female cousin.

Cousin

Place your *Y hand* on your temple and twist your hand forward and backward a couple of times. Think of the cow's horn.

Cow

Tap your fist on your elbow, as though you are "cracking" it.

Cracker

Use your bent 5 *hands* and snap them together like an alligator's jaw.

(Also see ALLIGATOR on page 157.)

Crocodile

Move your index fingers down your cheeks, showing tears falling.

Cry

Using your dominant hand, pretend you are holding on to a cup and tap it down onto your nondominant hand. Think of placing a cup onto a table.

Cup

Using your index and middle fingers, swipe them down your chin once.

Cute

Put the thumb of your 5 *hand* on your forehead, and wiggle your fingers a little, or you can tap your thumb on your forehead.

Daddy

Using your *V hand* in a "stand" position, move it back and forth, showing a dancing movement above your nondominant hand.

Dance

Hold your nondominant *A hand* near your chest and, moving your dominant *A hand* in front of it in a circular motion, tap it a couple of times. Think of blocking (nondominant hand) danger (dominant hand) coming at you.

Danger

Daughter is a combined sign of "girl" and "baby." Make the sign "girl" (page 201) and then "baby" (page 160).

Daughter

Hold your nondominant arm parallel to the ground, representing the horizon. Holding your index finger up, place your elbow on your hand and move your finger across the sky. Think of the sun moving across the sky during the day and finally setting.

Day

Using your index finger, point to where you would be wearing a diamond engagement ring.

Diamond

Tap your thumbs against your index and middle fingers on both hands, indicating where the pins of the diaper would be.

Diaper

Cross both index fingers together and then move them apart.

Different

Move your *D hand* along in front of you from one side to the other. Think of a dinosaur sauntering along.

Dinosaur

Place the back of your hand under your chin and wiggle your fingers. Think of crumbs falling from your dirty face.

Dirty

Tap the fingertips of your hand on your wrist as if you are testing your pulse. This sign can also be made by tapping the letter *d* on your wrist for doctor.

Doctor

Pat your leg, then snap your fingers. Usually with babies we just pat our leg. Think of how you would call a dog to you.

Dog

Using your *X hand* shape, move your finger down your nose twice.

Doll

Hold your nondominant hand flat like the surface of the water. Then, using your *D hand*, move it up and down with your index finger pointing up as you move your hand up and then point it down as you move it down. Think of a dolphin jumping up and down in the water.

Dolphin

Holding your hand in a fist, place your thumb under your chin and flick it outward while shaking your head no.

Don't

Place your thumb on the side of your head and bend your fingers up and down a couple of times. It's like the sign for horse, except it is made with all of your fingers.

Donkey

Hold your hands up in front of you beside each other with the backs of your hands facing you. Then flip your dominant hand so the palm is facing you. Think of a door opening and your pinky finger is the hinge.

Door

Simply point your finger down.

Down

Put your index finger on your head and then wiggle it outward as if a dream is coming out of your head.

Dream

Using your 5 *hands*, brush your thumbs down your chest and move your hands outward, showing the flowing fabric of a dress.

Dress

Using your 5 *hands*, run your thumbs down your chest a couple of times. Think of bringing attention to your clothes.

Dressed

Move your *C hand* to your mouth as if you are holding a glass and are about to take a drink.

Drink

Pretend you are holding on to drumsticks and are playing a drum.

Drum

Wipe your finger across your chin as if you are drying it off.

Dry

Put your hand up to your mouth and open and close it like a duck's bill opening and closing. Use your whole hand versus just index finger and thumb (bird), because a duck's bill is wider.

Duck

Bring your hand to your mouth as if you are putting food in it.

Eat

Holding your two *U hands* in front of you, middle fingers touching, move them down and apart. Think of an egg cracking apart.

Egg

Move your hand from your nose down as if you are outlining the trunk of the elephant.

Elephant

Using the middle fingers of your 5 *hands*, tap them upward on your chest. Think of how your excitement bubbles up in you.

Excited

Using a bent hand, brush your fingertips along the palm of your other hand.

Excuse me

F

Using both your *F hands*, draw a circle in front of you. Start by touching your index fingers and thumbs together, and then move your hands in a circle until your baby fingers are touching. Think of a family circle.

Family

Point your index finger up and move it in a circular motion. Think of showing the fan's blades moving around.

Fan

Using your 5 *hand*, drag your thumb across your chin. Think of a long fence in front of a farm.

Farm

Farmer

Sign "farm" (page 193), and then move both your hands down in front of your chest so they are facing each other. Moving your hands parallel to each other are people markers.

Finished

Put both hands up with your palms facing you, and then move your hands in a swift motion so that your palms are facing out. Repeat this motion a couple of times.

(Also see ALL DONE on page 156.)

Fire

Hold both 5 *hands* up with palms facing you, and then wiggle the fingers while moving your hands up and down. Think of the flickering flames of a fire.

Tap the back of your *B hand* on your forehead where the shield on the firefighter's hat would be.

Firefighter

Wiggle your flat hand while moving it forward, mimicking the swimming motion of a fish.

Fish

Place both hands flat in front of you, palms down, and move them out and away from each other. Think of showing the surface of a floor.

Floor

Using your *flattened O hand*, move your fingers from one side of your nose to another. Pretend you are delicately holding a flower and smelling it.

Flower

Using your *V hand* shape of your dominant hand, tap on the palm of your nondominant hand. Think of the prongs of a fork picking something up.

Fork

Put your *F hand* up to your nose and wiggle your fingers slightly. Think of a fox's long nose.

Fox

Using your *F hand,* palm facing you, make a circle in front of you.

Friday

Link your two index fingers together with your dominant hand on top, then change the positions of your hands so your nondominant hand is on top and link your fingers again. Think of giving your friend a big hug.

Friend

Place your index and middle fingers under your chin and flick out your fingers so they are straight. Do this movement a couple of times. Think of the throat of a bullfrog bulging out when it croaks.

Frog

Using your *F hand*, wiggle it slightly on your cheek. Think of placing it on the apple of your cheek.

Fruit

Tap the back of your right hand on your chin. Think of being so frustrated, it feels like you are walking into a brick wall.

Frustrated

Hold your nondominant hand in a fist and then move the palm of your dominant hand over your fist, showing that you could not fit anything else in your hand.

Full

Using your *U hand* shapes, touch your nose with your dominant hand and then touch your fingers down onto your nondominant hand.

Fun

Using the tips of your *U shape* hand, flick down on the end of your nose a couple of times.

Funny

Sign "flower" (page 196) and then "area" (page 158) together.

Garden

With your palms facing up, open and close your hands gently.

Gentle

Move one hand slowly up the back of the other hand.

Gently

Put your dominant hand at your neck and move it upward over your head. Think of showing a giraffe's long neck.

Giraffe

Slide the thumb from your *A hand* down your jaw, starting near your ear and ending near your chin. Think of drawing the line of the strap from a girl's bonnet.

Girl

Put your thumb and index finger in front of your eye where the glasses frame would be and move them outward and close to where the arm of the glasses would be.

Glasses

Point both of your fingers in the direction you want to go.

Go

Using a bent *V hand* shape, tap your hand on your chin and then move it up to your forehead. Think of showing the goat's beard and then its horns.

Goat

Place the fingertips of your flat dominant hand on your chin and then move your hand outward to tap into your nondominant hand. You can also just move your hand outward and not tap it into your other hand.

Good

Sign "good" (page 202) and then "morning" (page 225). Put your nondominant hand parallel to the ground, then take your other hand and bring it upward in front of you from under your nondominant arm. Think of a sun rising on the horizon.

Good morning

Sign "good" (page 202) and then "night" (page 228). Think of the sun setting below the horizon.

Good night

Place your 5 *hand* in the "mommy" position (page 222) and then bounce your hand forward twice. Think of showing the generations with each bounce forward.

Grandma

Place your 5 *hand* in the "daddy" position (page 182) and then bounce your hand forward twice. Think of showing the generations with each bounce forward.

Grandpa

Tap your fingers along the top of your hand, showing the bunches of grapes in a cluster.

Grapes

Tap your bent 5 *hand* on your chin. Think of your fingers being the blades of grass and your chin resting in them.

Grass

Using your 5 *hands* held at your head or higher, palms facing outward, pump your hands forward and backward twice.

Great

Shake or twist the wrist of your G *hand* just in front of you.

Green

Hold your 5 *hand* in front of your face and move your fingers in and out, showing your face scrunching up like a grouch.

(Also see ANGRY on page 157, MAD on page 220, or UPSET on page 281.)

Grumpy

This sign can be made using one or two hands. Tap your chest in an upward, circular motion.

(Also see MERRILY on page 221.)

Happy

Tap your head where a hat would be.

Hat

Hold up your thumb and index and middle fingers on your nondominant hand and place the palm of your other hand on top of your thumb, wiggling it a little. Think of the body and blades of the helicopter.

Helicopter

Putting your fist on top of your other flat hand, use your flat hand to "help" lift your fist up.

Help

Move your *A hand* under your nondominant hand as if you were hiding it.

Hide

Tap your thumb and baby finger from your dominant hand onto the corresponding fingers on your nondominant hand. Think of a hippo's mouth opening and closing and your fingers are the four big teeth.

Hippopotamus

Using your *flattened O hand,* touch the side of your mouth and then the top of your cheek. Think of a home being a place where you "eat" and "sleep."

Home

Using your *H hand* shape, put your thumb on the side of your forehead and move your fingers back and forth slightly, showing the horse's ear.

Horse

Place your hand at your mouth and then throw it away like you are throwing something hot from your mouth.

Hot

Use both hands to draw a shape of the roof and sides of a house.

House

Starting with the outside of your hands together, fingers pointing down, roll your hands up a little so your fingertips are facing you, then point out as if you are pointing at someone.

How are you?

Cross your arms in front of your chest and give a little squeeze just like you are giving yourself a hug.

(Also see LOVE on page 219.)

Hug

Using your C *hand*, drag it down your chest to your belly. Think of wanting to put food into your tummy.

(Also see WISH on page 288.)

Hungry

Tap your two index fingers together for hurt/pain. Position your hands over the area that hurts and make this sign. (For example, for a toothache, make this sign in front of your mouth.)

Hurt

Simply point at yourself.

I

Hold up your thumb, index, and baby fingers. You are holding up the letters *i* for I, *l* for love, and *y* for you all together to form "I love you."

I love you

Move your hand like you are licking an ice cream cone.

Ice cream

In/inside

Hold your nondominant hand in an *O hand* shape and place the *flattened O hand* of your dominant hand in it.

Use both hands and pretend you are pulling a coat up over your shoulders.

(Also see COAT *on page 176.)*

Jacket

Sign the letter *j* up near your mouth. Or you can sign "drink" and then the letter *j*.

Juice

Hold your nondominant hand flat with the palm facing up, representing the floor, and take the *V hand* shape of your dominant hand and jump it on your palm. It looks like a person jumping.

Jump

K

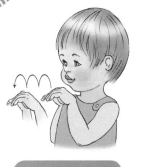

Hold your hands up in front of you with your fingertips pointing down. Bounce them forward a couple of times. Think of a kangaroo jumping.

Kangaroo

Take your *K hand* and move it from your left shoulder down to your right hip. Think of showing the sash that royalty would wear.

King

Touch the fingertips of your flat hand beside your mouth and move it up to your cheek. Think of taking a kiss from your mouth and placing it on your cheek.

Kiss

Flutter your dominant flat hand above your head, representing the kite, and then point the index finger of your nondominant hand as if it is the string of the kite. It looks like you are flying a kite.

Kite

Simply tap your head, indicating putting knowledge into your head.

Know

Lady

Make the sign "mommy" (page 222) and then move your hand down to tap your thumb on your chest.

(Also see WOMAN on page 289.)

Lane

Hold your hands parallel to each other and move them forward as if you are showing a road.

(Also see ROAD on page 249 or STREET on page 267.)

Large

Start with bent *L hands* close together and move them apart.

(Also see BIG on page 164.)

Hold the index finger of your two *L hands* at the corners of your mouth and wiggle them up and out as if you are showing laughter coming out of your mouth.

Laugh

Place your index finger on your wrist and then dangle your hand like a leaf on a twig.

Leaf

Move your two *L hands* up your chest.

Life

Hold your hands in a *flattened* O shape showing the light bulb, and then open your fingers, showing the light shining.

Light

Place your 5 *hand* on your chest and then pull your middle finger and thumb together so they are touching as you move your hand out. (This is not the sign "similar.")

Like

Move your hand along the top of your head like you are outlining the mane of a lion.

Lion

Hold your hands apart, palms facing each other, and then move them in toward each other, making the space between your hands smaller.

Little

Cross your arms in front of your chest and give a little squeeze just like you are giving yourself a hug.

(Also see HUG on page 209.)

Love

Hold your 5 *hand* in front of your face and move your fingers in and out, showing your face scrunching up like a grouch.

(Also see ANGRY *on page 157,* GRUMPY *on page 205, or* UPSET *on page 281.)*

Mad

Make the sign "daddy" (page 182) and then move your hand down to tap your thumb on your chest.

(Also see MASTER *on page 222 or* SIR *on page 258.)*

Man

Pinch the meaty part of your hand between your thumb and index finger and then sign "ball" (page 160).

Meatball

Wiggle the middle finger of your dominant 5 *hand* on your nondominant palm. Think of pointing to a pill on the palm of your hand.

Medicine

Hold your fists together and then drop them apart while you extend your thumbs out.

Melt

This sign can be made using one or two hands. Tap your chest in an upward, circular motion.

(Also see HAPPY on page 206.)

Merrily

Open and close your hand, using the same motion if you were to milk a cow.

Milk

Make the sign "daddy" (page 182) and then move your hand down to tap your thumb on your chest.

(*Also see* MAN *on page 220 or* SIR *on page 258.*)

Master

Using your 5 *hand,* put your thumb against your chin and wiggle your fingers a little, or you can tap your thumb on your chin.

Mommy

Using your *M hand* with palm facing in, move it in a circle in front of you.

Monday

Take your dominant *flattened O hand* and tap it into the palm of your nondominant hand. Pretend you are holding on to a big wad of cash and slapping it in your hand.

Money

Move your hands up and down as if you are a monkey scratching at your sides.

Monkey

Put both arms up and mimic the actions of a big monster.

Monster

Make the shape of the letter c, using only your index finger and thumb, and place it near your forehead, moving it up and out. Think of a crescent moon in the sky.

Moon

Put the thumbs of your 5 *hands* on your forehead and then move them up and out, showing the big antlers.

Moose

Using a *flattened O hand* shape, tap both hands together so that your fingertips are touching.

More

Put your nondominant hand parallel to the ground, then take your other hand and bring it upward in front of you from under your nondominant arm.

Morning

Flick the end of your nose a couple of times with your index finger. Think of a mouse's nose wiggling as it smells the air.

Mouse

Place your dominant hand with palm facing out against your nondominant hand. Move it back and forth a little, think of the flickering of a movie reel.

Movie

Move your hand up and down your arm as if you are conducting music.

(Also see SING on page 257 or SONG on page 263.)

Music

Tap your chest with your flat hand.

My

Shake your *N hand* up near your forehead. Boy signs are made above your nose.

Nephew

Take your dominant hand and pretend you are scooping something from your nondominant hand. Think of scooping up something new.

New

Brush the palm of your dominant hand forward along the palm of your nondominant hand.

Nice

Shake your *N hand* near the side of your chin. Girl signs are made below your nose.

Niece

Hold your nondominant hand flat with your palm facing down, and then cup your bent dominant hand on it. Think about the sun setting below the horizon when night comes.

Night

Using your index and middle fingers, tap them on your thumb a couple of times.

No

Using your baby fingers, move your hands apart as if you were tossing spaghetti noodles in a bowl.

(Also see PASTA on page 236 or SPAGHETTI on page 264.)

Noodle

Holding both your hands in the *Y hand* shape, palms facing you, drop them sharply down once.

Now

Hold your fingers and thumbs together in a *flattened O hand* shape on both hands. Tap them together once, then twist your wrists and tap them together again.

Number

Use the fingertips of your *N hand* to tap on your wrist. Think of a nurse checking your pulse.

Nurse

Sign "water" (page 285) and move your hands forward like you are mimicking the rolling waves.

(Also see SEA on page 253.)

Ocean

Put the fingertips of your left hand on top of the back of your right hand. Wiggle the fingers of your right hand like an octopus's tentacles wiggling in the water.

Octopus

Take your dominant flat hand off your nondominant hand.

Off

Sign the letter o and then *k*.

Okay

Take your hand and pull down at your chin. Think of pulling a long white beard.

Old

Place your dominant flat hand on your nondominant hand.

On

Hold your flat hands together, palms facing out, and then swing them both open, palms end up facing toward you. It looks like two cupboard doors opening.

Open

Open and close your hand in front of your mouth a couple of times like you are squeezing an orange.

Orange

Hold your nondominant hand in an *O hand* shape with the fingers and thumb of your dominant hand placed in it, then pull your hand out.

Out

Outside

Hold your hand in a loose 5 *hand* shape in front of your face and then move your hand out a little bit while closing your fingers and thumb together. Point your hand in the direction of outside.

Owl

Put both your O *hands* in front of your eyes and twist them a little. Think of highlighting the owl's big eyes.

Hold your index finger and thumb together and tap them on your mouth. Think of putting a pacifier into your mouth.

Pacifier

Use your *P hand* to draw a circle around your eye. Think of outlining the panda's black eyes.

Panda

Move your two parallel hands down one leg and then down your other one, showing the legs of the pants.

Pants

Sign "play" (page 240) and then sign "area" (page 158), moving your flat hand facing the ground in a small circle, showing the area in front of you.

PARK is often finger spelled P-A-R-K.

(Also see PLAYGROUND on page 241.)

Park

Hold your two *P hands* out in front of you and move them back and forth. Think of moving your hands like people dancing at a party.

Party

Using your baby fingers, move your hands apart as if you were tossing spaghetti noodles in a bowl.

(Also see NOODLE on page 229 or SPAGHETTI on page 264.)

Pasta

Pull gently at your cheek as if you are pulling your peach fuzz.

Peach

Hold your nondominant hand in a *flattened O hand* shape (representing a pear), then place the other hand on top of it. Pull your dominant hand off the "pear," outlining the shape as you do it.

Pear

Tap the letter *p* on your nose.

Pee

Pretend you are holding on to a pencil, then mime licking it and writing on a piece of paper.

Pencil

Use your dominant hand to pet your nondominant hand. Mimic the action of petting an animal.

Pet

Simply pretend you are playing the piano. Think of how you would play "air piano."

Piano

Using your C *hand*, place it in front of your face and then tap it onto the palm of your other hand. Think of taking a picture of your face and then hanging it on the wall.

Picture

Place your hand under your chin and wag your fingers up and down. Think of the drool falling from the pig's mouth.

Pig

This is actually a classifier rather than a sign. Hold your index finger up on your nondominant hand, representing the person, and then hook your index and middle finger from your dominant hand, representing the legs of the piggyback rider. It looks like a person giving someone a piggyback ride.

Piggyback

Place the middle finger of your *P hand* on the apple of your cheek and wiggle it a little.

Pineapple

Using the middle finger of your *P hand*, swipe it down on your bottom lip. Think of putting pink lipstick on.

Pink

Holding up your two *Y hands*, twist your wrists to make your *Y hands* dance.

Play

Sign "play" (page 240) and then sign "area" (page 158), moving your flat hand facing the ground in a small circle, showing the area in front of you.

(Also see PARK on page 236.)

Playground

Place your flat hand on your chest and move it in a circular motion.

Please

Tap your C *hand* twice on your left chest. Think of where a cop's badge would be.

Police

Take your nondominant hand and hold on to the thumb of your dominant hand. Then pull your thumb out of your nondominant hand. I think the memory tip here is self-explanatory.

Poop

Hold your nondominant hand in a fist. Then, using your index and middle fingers of your dominant hand, tap the top of the fist. Think of testing the doneness of a potato with a fork.

Potato

Using the *T hand* shape for "toilet," move your hand back and forth a few times.

(Also see TOILET *on page 276.)*

Potty

Using your 5 *hand,* hold it in front of your face, and then swipe your fingers around and down to your chin, closing your hand at the bottom. Think of showing how beautiful your face is.

(Also see BEAUTIFUL *on page 163.)*

Pretty

Hold your hand in a fist and, using your thumb, move it up from your belly to the top of your chest. Think of pride rising.

Proud

Open and close your hand as if you are moving the mouth of a puppet. Imagine having a puppet on your hand and you are making it talk.

Puppet

Shake or twist the wrist of your
P hand just in front of you.

Purple

Using your two *U hands,* tap your
fingertips together, then twist
your wrists so the opposite hand
is on top, and tap again. Do this
movement a few times. You are
showing the linking of the puzzle
pieces.

Puzzle

Take your Q *hand* and move it from your left shoulder down to your right hip. Think of showing the sash that royalty would wear.

Queen

Simply hold your finger in front of your mouth and make a "shhhh" sound.

Quiet

Rabbit

Hold up the index and middle fingers on both your hands, cross your hands in front of your chest, and wiggle your fingers a bit. Think of holding a bunny with its ears flopping.

(Also see BUNNY on page 170.)

Raccoon

Hold your *V hand* in front of both eyes and move them both outward as you close them. Think of the black "mask" on the raccoon's eyes.

Rain

Hold up both hands in front of you and drop them down, showing raindrops falling.

Rainbow

Move your *4 hand* in an arch, showing the stripes of the rainbow.

Rat

Flick your *R hand* on the end of your nose. Think of the rat's nose wiggling as it smells the air.

Read

Hold your nondominant hand flat, palm facing up, like it's a sheet of paper, and move your dominant *V hand* down the "page." Think of eyes moving while reading a page.

Recycle

Hold your two *R hands* with the fingertips pointing toward each other. Hold your nondominant hand in place while you draw a circle with your dominant hand. Think of the circle of the recycle sign.

Red

Move the tip of your index finger down your lips once, pointing to the color of your red lips.

Rhinoceros

Place the thumb of your *Y hand* on your nose and move your hand up and outward, showing the rhino's horn.

Hold your nondominant hand in the shape of a bowl and use your dominant *R hand* to pretend to scoop rice from the bowl up to your mouth.

Rice

Hold your hands parallel to each other and move them forward as if you are showing a road.

(Also see LANE on page 216 or STREET on page 267.)

Road

Tap one fist on top of the other like you are tapping two rocks together.

Rock

Using your number 3 *hand,* place the thumb on your forehead. Think of showing the crown of a rooster.

Rooster

Holding your two hands in the *L hand* shape, hook the index finger of your dominant hand onto the thumb of your nondominant hand. Then bend and straighten your nondominant index finger as you move your hands forward.

Run

Place your flat hand in front of your face and drag it down slightly, making a sad face. Think of your face dropping down when you frown.

Sad

Using your *Y hand*, move it back and forth in front of you. That is the general sign for talking about the same thing. You can also direct the sign toward something that is the same.

Same

Using your dominant hand, hold on to the fingers of your nondominant hand and put it to your mouth, pretending you are eating a sandwich.

Sandwich

Using your *S hand*, palm facing you, move it in a circle in front of you.

Saturday

Start with your hands held tightly in *S hand* shapes and then thrust your hands toward each other, opening them up into a 5 *hands* shape, as if you were just startled.

Scared

Clap your two hands together. Think of a schoolteacher clapping her hands to get the students' attention.

School

Sign "water" (page 285) and move your hands forward like you are mimicking the rolling waves.

(Also see OCEAN on page 231.)

Sea

Using your *V hand*, place your middle finger on your face close to your eye and then move it outward.

See

Twist your index finger on your chin.

Serious

Share

Hold your nondominant flat hand up with your palm facing your body. Place your other hand on top of it and slide that hand back and forth up your index finger and toward your thumb. Think some for you (as you sweep out toward your fingertip) and some for me (as you sweep in toward your thumb).

Sheep

Hold your nondominant arm up as if you are holding a sheep, and use your dominant *V hand,* palm facing you, opening and closing it as you move it up your arm. Think of holding on to a sheep and cutting its wool.

Shine

Place the middle finger of your 5 *hand* on the back of your nondominant hand. Wiggle it up and out, showing shining coming off your skin.

(Also see TWINKLE on page 279.)

Use your index finger and thumb to pull at your shirt. (This sign can also mean "volunteer.")

Shirt

Tap your two fists together; your thumb and index fingers should be connecting. Think of Dorothy in *The Wizard of Oz* tapping her shoes together to get home.

Shoes

Move your bent 5 *hand* away from your mouth as if you are throwing words out.

Shout

Shower

Hold your hand above your head with your fingers and thumb held together, and then open your hand up as you move it downward slightly. Think of the water from the shower falling onto your head.

Shy

Put the back of your fingers on your cheek and roll your hand slightly forward. Think of your cheeks getting flushed when you are shy.

Sick

Using your 5 *hand* shapes, touch your middle fingers to your forehead (dominant hand) and your tummy (nondominant hand) at the same time.

Sign

Hold your two index fingers up and move both hands in a circular motion. Think of pretending to sign something.

Silly

Using your *Y hand*, tap the end of your nose from side to side with your thumb.

Sing

Move your hand up and down your arm as if you are conducting music.

(Also see MUSIC on page 226 or SONG on page 263.)

Sir

Make the sign "daddy" (page 182) and then move your hand down to tap your thumb on your chest.

(Also see MAN on page 220 and MASTER on page 222.)

Sister

Using two *L hand* shapes, touch your chin with the thumb of your dominant hand where the sign "girl" is made and then move it down to tap on your nondominant *L hand*.

Sit

Tap your *U hand* shape down on your other *U hand* once. Think of setting one hand down on the other one.

Using your flat hand above your head, palm facing down, move it "across" the sky.

Sky

Hold your 5 *hand* in front of your face and move it down to your chin while closing your fingers together. Think of your eyes closing when you are sleepy.

Sleep

Flutter your fingertips in front of your face a couple of times. Think of eyes fluttering when they are sleepy.

(Also see TIRED on page 274.)

Sleepy

Using your *U hand* shapes, slide one *U* down the other one. Think of a child going down the slide.

Slide

Move one hand slowly up the back of the other hand.

Slow

Place the middle finger of your *5 hand* on the side of your head and move it up and out. Think of your brain waves exploding from your head.

(Also see CLEVER on page 177.)

Smart

Place your index fingers on the sides of your mouth and draw the shape of a smile.

Smile

Start with your hand near your mouth with your index and middle fingers in the shape of a snake's tongue. Move your hand away from your mouth in an S motion. Think of a snake slithering away.

Snake

Put your index finger under your nose and pretend to sneeze.

Sneeze

Similar to the sign "rain," except you wiggle your fingers as you drop your hands down, showing the snowflakes fluttering down.

Snow

Point your two index fingers down toward the floor and move them up and down as they brush together. Think of pulling your socks onto your feet.

Socks

This is a combined sign of "boy" and "baby" together. Make the sign "boy" (page 168) and then "baby" (page 160).

Son

Song

Move your hand up and down your arm as if you are conducting music.

(Also see MUSIC on page 226 or SING on page 257.)

Sorry

Move your fist on your chest in a circular motion.

Soup

Holding your nondominant hand in the shape of a bowl, use your dominant *U hand* to pretend to scoop soup from the bowl up to your mouth.

Spaghetti

Using your baby fingers, move your hands apart as if you were tossing spaghetti noodles in a bowl.

(Also see NOODLE *on page 229 or* PASTA *on page 236.)*

Spider

Cross your hands over each other at the wrists and wiggle your fingers like you are mimicking a spider's legs moving.

Spring

Use your nondominant C *hand* to represent the ground, and using your dominant *flattened* O *hand*, move it up through the ground while spreading your fingers open, representing a growing flower.

Squirrel

Bend the index and middle fingers of both hands and tap them together. Think of the squirrel's teeth chattering together.

Stand

Stand your upside down *V hand* shape on the palm of your other hand.

Star

Point your index fingers up and move them slightly up and down as if you are pointing at the stars in the sky.

Start

Hold your nondominant hand flat with your palm facing toward you, and then place the index finger of your dominant hand between your index and middle fingers. Make a twisting movement like you are turning a key in a lock. Think of putting a key in the car's ignition and starting it.

(Also see BEGIN on page 164.)

Stop

Move your dominant hand down in a swift chopping motion onto your nondominant palm.

Store

Holding your fingers and thumb together, point both hands down and shake them forward twice. Think of holding on to two wads of cash and giving them away as you shop.

Strawberry

Using your dominant hand, hold on to the end of your nondominant index finger and twist a little. Think of twisting off the green stem.

Stream

Wiggle your fingers as you move your hands forward, mimicking water flowing down the stream.

Street

Hold your hands parallel to each other and move them forward as if you are showing a road.

(Also see LANE on page 216 or ROAD on page 249.)

Stroller

Pretend you are holding on to the handle of a stroller and mimic rocking it forward twice.

Summer

Bend your index finger as you move it across your forehead like you are wiping sweat from your brow.

Sun

Hold your *C hand* near your forehead and then move your hand up and out slightly.

Hold your flat hands up with palms facing out, and then drop them down.

Sunday

Put your index fingers and thumbs together right in front of your eyes. Then move your fingers apart, mimicking your eyes opening. Think of your eyes popping open when you are surprised.

Surprise

Wipe your fingers down your chin. Think of wiping off sweet sugar that fell on your chin.

Sweet

"Sweet" (page 269) + "potato" (page 242) = sweet potato.

Sweet potato

Move your hands like you are mimicking doing a small breaststroke in the water.

Swim

Hook your dominant *U hand* over your nondominant *U hand* and swing your hands forward.

Swing

Tap one arm on top of the other to show the surface of the table.

Table

Using your *4 hand,* tap your index finger on your mouth. Think of words coming out of your mouth as you speak.

Talk

Place your *flattened O hands* against your forehead and move them forward, making the sign "teach." Then drop your hands down so the palms are facing each other; these are people markers.

Teacher

Using your *Y hand* shape, hold your thumb up to your ear and your baby finger near your mouth. It looks like you are talking on a phone.

Telephone

Simply sign the letters *t* and *v*.

Television

Place your fingertips on your chin and then move your hand out and down.

Thank you

Using your index finger, draw a line down your throat. Think of how parched your throat feels when you are thirsty.

Thirsty

Hold your hand like you have a ball in it, and move your hand forward as though you were mimicking throwing a ball.

Throw

Make the letters *t* and *h* for the TH in Thursday.

Thursday

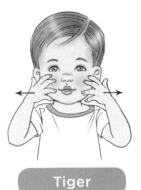

Holding your hands in claw shapes, move them across your face showing the tiger's stripes.

Tiger

Point to your wrist where your watch would be.

Time

Put your fingertips on your chest and then drop your arms down as if you are too tired to hold them up.

(Also see SLEEPY on page 259.)

Tired

Hold your nondominant hand flat, palm facing you, representing a piece of bread. Then using your *V hand,* pretend to stick it into both sides of the bread, first one side, then the other. Think of toasting a piece of bread over an open fire.

Toast

Holding both your hands in the *Y hand* shape, palms facing you, bounce them down twice.

Today

Hold both fists together and move both hands in a circle.

Together

Toilet

Using the *T hand* shape for "toilet," move your hand back and forth a few times.

(Also see POTTY on page 242.)

Tomato

Hold your nondominant hand in a *flattened O hand* shape. Using the index finger with your dominant hand, make the sign "red" (page 248). Then pretend to chop down along your fingertips. Think of cutting a "red" tomato.

Toothbrush

Using your index finger, mimic the motion of brushing your teeth.

Shake or twist your *T hands*. This is the same movement as the sign "play." Make sure to use two hands, as using only one is "toilet."

Toy

Both hands are in a *U hand* shape and the dominant hand moves forward and back along the "tracks" of the nondominant hand.

Train

Hold your nondominant arm out, representing the ground, and place your dominant elbow on your hand with your 5 *hand* up. Twist your wrist showing a tree blowing in the wind.

Tree

Move your hands like you are driving a big truck.

Truck

Using your *T hand*, palm facing you, move it in a circle in front of you.

Tuesday

Hold your *L hand* with the palm facing down, and then flip your hand over so your palm is facing up. Think of the thumb pointing first at you and then flipping over to someone else, showing that it is now their turn.

Turn (taking turns)

Turtle

Cover your *A hand* with your curved hand and wiggle your thumb a little. Your thumb looks like a turtle's head sticking out of its shell.

Twinkle

Place the middle finger of your *5 hand* on the back of your nondominant hand. Wiggle it up and out, showing shining coming off your skin.

(Also see SHINE on page 254.)

Umbrella

Holding both hands in fists, place your dominant hand on top of your nondominant one and move it upward to make the motion of opening an umbrella.

Uncle

Holding your *U hand* up near your forehead, move it in a circular motion. You can also make a twisting motion at the wrist.

Understand

Hold your hand up near your forehead in a fist and then flick your index finger up. Think of a light bulb coming on when you understand something.

Simply point your finger up.

Up

Hold your 5 *hand* in front of your face and move your fingers in and out, showing your face scrunching up like a grouch.

(Also see ANGRY on page 157, GRUMPY on page 205, or MAD on page 220.)

Upset

Move your hands like you are driving a car.

Van is normally finger spelled V-A-N, but for babies we often just sign car (page 173).

Van

Place the index finger of your *V hand* on the side of your mouth and wiggle it a little.

Vegetable

Pretend you are holding on to the handle of a wagon and are giving it a little tug.

Wagon

Holding both 5 *hands* up with palms facing you, wiggle your fingers a bit. Think of feeling fidgety when you have to wait for someone.

Wait

Hold both flat hands parallel to the ground palms facing down and "walk" your hands forward a bit.

Walk

Want

Put your hands out with your hands facing up and pull them in while bending your fingers toward you. Think of grabbing something that you want.

Warm

Put your loose 5 *hand* in front of your face and blow on your fingers as you move them outward away from your mouth. Think of putting something hot up to your mouth and you are trying to blow on it to make it cooler.

Wash

Hold both hands in fists and rub the top hand in a circular motion. Think of holding on to a dirty shirt and you are trying to scrub out a stain.

Tap the index finger of your *W hand* shape on the edge of your mouth.

Water

Using your *W hand*, palm facing you, move it in a circle in front of you.

Wednesday

Hold your dominant hand out in front of you with your palm facing up and pull it in toward your belly. Think of welcoming something to you.

(*Also see* YOU'RE WELCOME *on page 293.*)

Welcome

Wet

Hold both hands with your palms up in a loose 5 *hands* shape, and then drop your hands a little while closing your fingers and thumb together. Think of pulling water out of a hanging towel.

Whale

Wave your *Y hand* up and down a few times while moving it in front of your body. Think of a whale's tail rising and falling in the water.

What

Hold both hands open with palms facing up, shrug your shoulders, and wiggle your hands a bit from side to side.

Hold your index finger up and wag it back and forth.

Where

Place the fingertips of your 5 *hand* on your chest and then pull your hand away from your chest and move your fingers together.

White

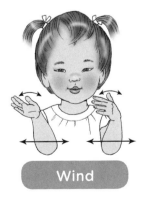

Move your hands back and forth, showing the wind blowing.

Wind

Hold both hands flat with palms facing you. Place your dominant hand on top of your nondominant hand and mimic a window opening.

Window

Holding your hands in fists and your arms close to your body, shiver like you are cold.

(Also see COLD on page 178.)

Winter

Using your C *hand*, drag it down your chest.

(Also see HUNGRY on page 210.)

Wish

Woman

Make the sign "mommy" (page 222) and then move your hand down to tap your thumb on your chest.

(Also see LADY on page 216.)

Wonder

Hold your index finger up near your head and move it in a circular motion. Think of the thoughts circling around of your head as you are wondering about something.

Work

This sign is similar to "rock." Place one fist on top of the other. Think of the sayings "a hard day's work" and "nose to the grindstone."

Hold both hands in a *W hand* shape. Place your dominant hand on top of your nondominant one and then move it in a circle around it. Think of the rotation of the earth.

World

Move your index finger along the palm of your hand like a wiggling worm.

Worm

X

Xylophone

Pretend you are holding on to sticks and are playing the xylophone from one end to the other.

Yellow

Shake or twist the wrist of your *Y hand* just in front of you.

Yes

Using your *S hand,* shake it up and down in the same way you would move your head when nodding yes.

Yogurt

Hold your nondominant hand in the shape of a cup and then, using your *Y hand,* dip your thumb in the "cup" and move it up to your mouth. (I have also seen this sign done with dipping the baby finger in the "cup.") This is a new sign, so "yogurt" is also often finger spelled.

Simply point at "someone."

You

Hold your dominant hand out in front of you with your palm facing up and pull it in toward your belly. Think of welcoming something to you.

(Also see WELCOME on page 285.)

You're welcome

Zebra

Using your clawed 5 *hands,* draw stripes a few times along your chest. Think of the zebra's stripes.

Zoo

Simply spell out the word "zoo," but do it in a smooth fluid motion, Z-O-O.

Acknowledgments

I would like to thank my amazing agent, Daphne Hart of the Helen Heller Agency, for always believing in me and being so helpful, supportive, and kind throughout this journey. Without you there would be no book. I also want to thank Linda Pruessen, who was a fantastic set of second eyes for my book and offered great suggestions. And a huge thank-you to my assistant, Ina Zubaite, who came into my life to take care of me, my business, and my children while I wrote this book. Without your love and support and total dedication to my family and me, I could not have done it.

And a big thanks to my friends, family, and the My Smart Hands team of instructors who believed in me and supported me always.

Last, thank you to Avery (Penguin) Publishing and the amazing people there who worked with me on this book, for allowing me to write for your company. I am honored.

Resources

· ·

My Smart Hands

www.mysmarthands.com

A great resource for all things baby sign language is the My Smart Hands Web site. Here you will discover fun games you can play with your baby, as well as classes in your area.

The Baby Signing Expert Blog

www.babysignlanguageexpert.com

A weekly post on all things baby sign language, you'll find great information and resources to help you in your baby-signing endeavor.

The Baby Signing Bible

www.mysmarthands.com/babysigningbible

This site provides updated information or resources to accompany the book. It includes author book signings where you can come meet Laura Berg in person.

Baby Sign Language Facebook Group

http://www.facebook.com/MySmartHandsFan

This is a great group where you will meet other parents who share the same interest in signing with babies. You can post questions, share stories, read others' stories, and get support, if needed. This is an engaging and interactive group. It is monitored either by the author of this book or one of her instructors. If you post a question here, someone will answer it.

American Academy of Pediatrics

http://www.aap.org

Canadian Paediatric Society

http://www.cps.ca

These Web sites have great information about infant development and pediatric care in your area.

American Speech-Language-Hearing Association

http://www.asha.org/

Canadian Association of Speech-Language Pathologists and Audiologists

http://www.caslpa.ca

Information on finding a speech and language pathologist

References

....

Bloom, Lois. *The Transition from Infancy to Language: Acquiring the Power of Expression*. Cambridge: Cambridge University Press, 1993.

Bullowa, M., ed. *Before Speech: The Beginning of Interpersonal Communication*. New York: Cambridge University Press, 1979.

Daniels, M. *Dancing with Words: Signing for Hearing Children's Literacy*. Westport, CT: Bergin and Garvey, 2001.

Field, T. M., and T. A. Walden. "Production and Perception of Facial Expressions in Infancy and Early Childhood." *Advances in Child Development and Behavior* 16, (1982), pp. 169–211.

Garcia, Joseph. *Sign with Your Baby: How to Communicate with Infants Before They Can Speak*. Sign2Me Early Learning/Northlight Communications; Revised, ASL-English Edition (March 1, 2002).

Gibbs, Betsy, and Ann Springer. *Early Use of Total Communication: An Introductory Guide for Parents*. Baltimore: Paul H. Brookes Publishing, 1995.

Mitchell, Ross E., Travas A. Young, Bellamie Bachleda, and Michael A. Karchmer. "How Many People Use ASL in the United States? Why Estimates Need Updating." Gallaudet Research Institute— Gallaudet University, *Sign Language Studies* 6, no. 3 (2006), pp. 306–35.

Morris, Rick. *Using Sign Language in the Classroom.* New Management. http://www.newmanagement.com/index.html.

Stokoe, William C. "Sign Language Structure: An Outline of the Visual Communication Systems of the American Deaf," *Studies in Linguistics: Occasional Papers,* no. 8. Buffalo, NY: Department of Anthropology and Linguistics, University of Buffalo, 1960.

"What Is Child Development and What Skills Do Children Develop at Different Ages?" http://www.kidscrossing.com/documents/ChildDevelopment_000.pdf.

Research Reports and Articles

This is a long research paper but has great points on signing with babies, as well as links to other research at the end.

http://mysmarthands.com/Site/Baby_Sign_Language_Research_Paper.html

This report will summarize various research findings that have demonstrated how hearing children successfully learned to read or improve their reading skills with the use of signing and finger spelling.

http://www.pbs.org/teachers/earlychildhood/articles/signlanguage.html

How the brain develops

http://www.pbs.org/newshour/bb/youth/jan-june97/brain_5-29.html

People who learn sign language from birth use a region of the brain that those who learn to sign later in life can't access.

http://web.archive.org/web/20020126214900/health.yahoo
.com/search/healthnews?lb=s&p=id:7021

Six-month-old hearing infants exposed to American Sign Language for the first time prefer it to pantomime, lending new evidence that humans show a broad preference for languages over "non-languages."
http://www.washington.edu/news/archive/id/2407.html

A baby's brain can process language as early as three months of age, a French study suggests.
http://www.healthscout.com/template.asp?page=newsdetail&
ap=1&id=510662

A growing number of parents and children have begun using American Sign Language as part of their daily communication. Some day care centers even incorporate sign language into their daily curriculums.
http://www.intelihealth.com/IH/ihtIH/WSIHW000/3324
/29698.html#2

As part of a pilot program at an Ohio State University laboratory school, infants as young as nine months old and their teachers have learned to use sign language.
http://www.newswise.com/articles/view/10852

Teaching sign language to young students who can hear boosts their ability to read.
http://www.healthscout.com/template.asp?page=newsdetail&
ap=1&id=109892&pageNum=1

Index

Manual alphabet, (*cont.*)

   reading skills and, 97–103

   see also Finger spelling

Martha's Vineyard Sign Language
   (MVSL), 4–5

Meaning of signs, 94

   realization of, 75–77

Memory enhancement, 99

   music and, 115

Mexico, 8

Milestones. *See* Developmental
   milestones

Motivational signs, 87–88, 131

Motor functions

   developmental milestones in, 51

   disorders of, 40

My Smart Hands, ix, xii, 107, 296

Names, signs for, 130–31

Narrating your day, 59, 61, 90

National Institute for Child Health and
   Human Development, 24

National Institute for Deaf-Mutes, 4

National Institutes of Health, 24

Needs, anticipating and responding to,
   85–86

Negative social behaviors, 39

Newman, Aaron J., 19

Numbers, signs for, 146

   songs and, 122

Observation, 75

Ohio State University, 300

Opposite pairs, 133-34

Oregon, University of, 19

Outdoor time, 80, 127–28, 139

Peabody Picture Vocabulary Test
   (PPVT-R), 98

Pediatric Association, 44

Peekaboo games, 55, 130

Penn State University, 97

Phonics, 100–101

Photo albums, family, 130

Potty training, 105

Preschools, signing in, 43, 97–99, 113

Reading

   acquiring skills in, benefits of signing
     for, 76, 97–99, 101–3, 124–25,
     299, 300

   to babies and toddlers, 53, 55, 56, 58,
     60, 61

Repetition of signs, 82–84

Right angular gyrus, 19

Routines, incorporating signs into,
   77–78, 103–5

Seasons, signs for, 151–52

   books and, 135–36

Self-esteem, 19–21, 27

Sentences, 47–48, 73

   in apraxia, 41–42

   babbling in, 36, 56

   in foreign languages, 48–49

   speaking in, early, 32, 34

   structure of, in English versus ASL 3,
     9, 10, 104

Sesame Street, 8, 71

Shriver, Eunice Kennedy, National
     Institute for Child Health and
     Human Development, 24

Signing

   avoiding frustration through having
     fun with, 108–9

   branching out, 91–105

   building on basics, 94–95

   eye contact and, 106–7

About the Author

....

Laura Berg is the founder of My Smart Hands, "Educating Young Minds," an international company that teaches sign language to hearing children. Berg started the company in 2005 as its only instructor, and in just a few short years has grown it into a huge international organization. It now has instructors across North America and as far away as Spain, South Africa, Japan, Germany, the Philippines, and more.

Berg has an undergraduate degree in sociology and child studies from the University of Guelph, a master of education from Daemen College in New York, and an ASL and deaf studies certificate from George Brown College.

Berg's educational background and practical experience make her one of the leading experts in baby sign language. She has posted close to 400 videos on the subject on YouTube and has had nearly 18 million views. She lectures across the continent on the benefits of using sign language with hearing children. Thousands of families around the world have learned from Berg's My Smart Hands program and resources.

Berg lives in Toronto with her husband and two children.